William Holden Hutton

The Marquess Wellesley, K.G. and the Development of the

Company into the Supreme Power in India

William Holden Hutton

The Marquess Wellesley, K.G. and the Development of the Company into the Supreme Power in India

ISBN/EAN: 9783337812164

Printed in Europe, USA, Canada, Australia, Japan

Cover: Foto ©ninafisch / pixelio.de

More available books at **www.hansebooks.com**

From the picture by J. Hoppner, R.A.

The Marquess Wellesley, K.G.

*AND THE DEVELOPMENT OF THE COMPANY
INTO THE SUPREME POWER IN INDIA*

BY THE

REV. W. H. HUTTON, B.D.

FELLOW AND TUTOR OF S. JOHN'S COLLEGE, OXFORD

THIRD THOUSAND

Oxford

AT THE CLARENDON PRESS: 1897

PREFACE

THE life of Wellesley has still to be written on a scale proportionate to the greatness of the subject. Three well-known biographies exist. Mr. Pearce's (3 vols., Bentley, 1846) is too often verbose and trivial. Mr. Macullagh Torrens's brilliant 'historic portrait' (Chatto and Windus, 1880) does not profess to be systematic. Colonel Malleson's sketch (W. H. Allen & Co., 1889) is—it is its only fault—too brief. Till the time shall come when a complete memorial of the great statesman shall be undertaken by one qualified alike to estimate and to portray, shorter studies, it is hoped, may be permitted: and among these may this attempt, however unworthy, find place.

The authorities for the subject are very numerous. Without mentioning the sources of information on particular campaigns and particular personages, references to which will be found in the notes, I may name among general histories those of Captain Grant Duff, Colonel Wilks, Sir John Malcolm, and Mr. James Mill. The last work is one on which, in spite of the elements of greatness it possesses, it would be rash indeed to rely either for facts or principles.

Mr. Montgomery Martin's *Despatches, Minutes, and Correspondence of the Marquess Wellesley* (W. H. Allen & Co., second edition, 1840) are absolutely indispensable to any student of the great Governor-General. Mr. Sidney Owen's selection from these (Clarendon Press, 1878) is wholly admirable and has won deserved popularity. Other letters are found printed in different books,—some interesting ones of a personal nature, for instance, in the lives by Mr. Pearce and Mr. Torrens, and others in Mr. G. W. Forrest's *Selections from the Letters, Despatches, and other State Papers preserved in the Bombay Secretariat, Marátha Series*, vol. i, Bombay, 1885.

The unprinted material is, I think, nearly as important as that already published. The Manuscripts of Mr. Fortescue, preserved at Dropmore, have been examined for the Historical MSS. Commission, and the first volume of the report has been published (1892). It is exceedingly valuable, and I have made much use of it. In the British Museum there are nearly 400 volumes given by the representatives of Lord Wellesley. Among these are two volumes of letters to the Select Committee, 1798–1803; a volume containing a statement of the Secret Service money expended, 1799–1805; twenty-seven volumes of private and official correspondence (much of this has been printed); drafts of letters to be sent, but for the most part not despatched; minutes on the finances of India; papers, reports, and books relative to the household establishment and expenses of the Governor-General; and a number of letters and papers for the period 1808-22.

In the Record Department of the India Office there is also a great mass of MS. material, most of which has, so far as I can see, been used by none of Wellesley's biographers. There repose all the Court Minutes of the East India Company, their despatches to Bengal and the replies thereto, the proceedings of the Government in India for the period, and twenty-four volumes of Wellesley's papers, containing letters from Madras and Bombay to the Governor-General. A number of separate collections, such as the Fisher papers and the Miscellaneous Records, contain much matter of great value. Of some of these collections printed catalogues exist. Sir Henry Waterfield drew up a rough list of an enormous mass of documents on subjects relating to politics and trade, which was printed in 1875. Of others there are only MS. catalogues, and these do not profess to be complete. I am greatly indebted to the kindness of officials of the Record Department for their assistance to me during the researches I was allowed to make at the India Office. I have made considerable use of the MS. material, and I believe that some extracts, such as the opinions of Wellesley and Dundas on the re-arrangement of Indian administration (pp. 113-115), and of Warren Hastings on the education of Civil Servants (pp. 123-124), will be found of much interest.

I am very greatly indebted to my friend, the Rev. Roland Allen, who has done me the great kindness to read my proofs and give me the benefit of valuable criticism; and I have also to thank Mr. Reginald Van Wart for friendly aid. Nor can I refrain from acknowledging my debt to the courtesy and patience of the Editor of this series as well as to his unrivalled knowledge of India.

CONTENTS

CHAP.		PAGE
I.	Birth and Training	11
II.	Beginnings in India : the Nizám ; the Presidencies	21
III.	The Conquest of Mysore	31
IV.	The Karnátik ; Tanjore ; Oudh	56
V.	Wellesley and the Maráthás	82
VI.	Government ; Education ; Defence	111
VII.	Finance ; Trade ; Quarrels with the Directors	144
VIII.	Later Life	165
IX.	The Great Proconsul : his Fame and Achievements	192

NOTE

The orthography of proper names follows the system adopted by the Indian Government for the *Imperial Gazetteer of India*. That system, while adhering to the popular spelling of very well-known places, such as Punjab, Poona, Deccan, &c., employs in all other cases the vowels with the following uniform sounds :—

a, as in woman : *á*, as in father : *i*, as in kin : *í*, as in intrigue : *o*, as in cold : *u*, as in bull : *ú*, as in rule.

THE MARQUESS WELLESLEY

CHAPTER I

Birth and Training

On the roll of British Rulers of India there is no greater name than that of Richard Marquess Wellesley. Warren Hastings alone, among his predecessors, can claim to be his equal: among his successors it would be difficult to find a superior. As an administrator and a statesman, alike in his projects and in his achievements, he stands out unmistakably among the greatest men of his age; and it is in far distant times and amid wholly different circumstances that we must seek, if we are to point to triumphs more extensive than his. It is ill comparing the trophies of heroes: but if it was Clive who won and Hastings who preserved the English foothold in the great peninsula, it was Wellesley incontestably who founded the British Empire in the East. He found the East India Company a trading body: he left it, almost in spite of itself, the mightiest power in the land.

The genealogies of great men are often an arid and

unprofitable study: but a peculiar interest attaches to the ancestry of Wellesley. From what strain was it that the four brothers, all men of mark and two of undoubted genius, derived their powers? We have no satisfactory answer. An ancient family of Irish gentlemen, giving birth in one of its branches to the great religious leader of the eighteenth century, the house of Wesley—it had once, when spelling was more irregular, been Wellesley or Wellesleigh—had thriven for centuries respectably, if without any remarkable distinction. Garret Wesley, a friend and neighbour of Swift, lived blamelessly and died without issue. Charles Wesley, the 'sweet singer' of Methodism, might, if he would, have been his heir. When he declined, another kinsman, Richard Colley of Castle Carbery, was adopted, and in due time succeeded to the name and the estates. His service to the government, which appears to have been slight, or the position of his family, received recognition in the grant of a peerage: in 1746 Richard Colley Wesley became Baron Mornington in the peerage of Ireland. He was himself something of a virtuoso: his son Garret Wesley was a musician of no inconsiderable note. It was uncommon then to see a peer, even an Irish peer, as leader of the Orchestra; but the second Lord Mornington was respected as a man, and admired —he is still remembered—as a musician. He married in 1759 Anne, daughter of Arthur Hill Trevor, afterwards Lord Dungannon, and in the same year was raised to the rank of an earl.

The eldest son of a talented musician and an accomplished woman, Richard Colley Wesley [1] was born at Dangan Castle, County Meath, on June 20, 1760. His brothers, William, afterwards Earl of Maryborough, Arthur, the great Duke of Wellington, and Henry, best known as Lord Cowley and British Ambassador at Paris, were born in 1763, 1769 and 1773 respectively. His mother when, one day in her old age, her carriage was delayed in the street by an applauding crowd, said to her youngest son with pardonable pride, 'This comes of being the mother of the Gracchi.'

Richard, after some country schooling at Trim, was sent to Harrow, whence he shortly departed under such stigma as attached to those boys who joined in barring out a new Head Master, one Heath from Eton, because they preferred a certain Samuel Parr, who was to become famous when Heath was forgotten. In consequence of this escapade the little rebel of eleven was transferred to Eton, which he ever afterwards loved with all the devotion of a convert. There he acquired that accurate knowledge of the Greek and Latin classics and that singular facility in composition which marked him through life. An enthusiastic but critical judge, Dr. Goodall, afterwards Head Master of Eton, considered him easily Porson's

---

[1] It is said that Richard Wesley began to spell his name Wellesley when he was at Eton. He was matriculated at Oxford as Wellesley. His brother Arthur spelled his name Wesley till much later. Many of his Indian despatches are so signed.

superior as a scholar. He was in the same house with his brother Arthur. William Grenville and Sir John Newport, two of his schoolfellows, were his constant friends through life. It is said[1] that at the Speeches in 1777 he recited Strafford's speech with such pathos that George III shed tears, and that when he returned, as he often did, with Archbishop Cornwallis to Lambeth, he saw Garrick, who said, 'Your Lordship has done what I never could do; you have drawn tears from the King.' 'Yes,' answered Wesley, 'but you never spoke before him in the character of a fallen, favourite, arbitrary minister.'

From Eton he went in December 1778 to Christ Church[2]. In 1780 he won the Chancellor's prize for Latin verse, the subject being the death of Captain Cook. In the next year his father died, and it fell to him to pay his debts and educate his children. The task was performed with honour and success.

As a member of the Irish House of Peers, in Grattan's time, the young Lord Mornington's talents soon commanded attention. When his friend William Grenville became Chief Secretary for Ireland, the correspondence between them became constant, and was concerned with matters of political importance. Mornington was exceedingly active. 'I shall be happy and proud,'

---

[1] *Quarterly Review*, vol. cxlix. p. 364.
[2] 'Being unanimously elected by the Dean and Chapter a student of that institution.' Marquess Wellesley, *Primitiae et Reliquiae*, p. 34.

he wrote to Grenville, 'to take a decided part with you in and out of Parliament; and shall, with the greatest readiness, contribute anything within the compass of my abilities to the success of your plans, and to the arrangement of them. In short, I shall deem it a very small tribute paid to that constant, uniform, and ardent friendship which has so often assisted me in every shape, to devote myself to the use of a government proceeding on pure principles. ... You may consider me as one of your assistant secretaries, a servant though not a slave of the crown; and ready to fag with you at business as we used to fag at Lent verses and Episco-pastorals together[1].' His private letters contain vivid descriptions of the disturbed life of the Irish Parliament. In 1784 he entered the English House of Commons as one of the two members for the borough of Beeralston, a seat which he exchanged in 1788 for that of Windsor, and for Old Sarum in 1796. He was soon recognised as a man of capacity and power. He was one of the original knights on the creation of the Order of St. Patrick, and in 1786 was made a Lord of the Treasury. His earlier political attachments were all of a liberal complexion. He was a warm admirer of Grattan[2] and became an intimate friend of Pitt, of whose commercial proposals for Ireland he

---

[1] Hist. MSS. Commission. Dropmore MSS., vol. i. p. 164.

[2] In a letter to W. Grenville he speaks of him as 'the first of all men in ability and virtue, my friend Grattan.' Hist. MSS. Commission. Dropmore MSS., vol. i. p. 164.

was a strong supporter. He opposed in 1789 the request of the Irish Parliament to the Prince of Wales to assume the office of Regent with unlimited powers. He was in complete sympathy with Wilberforce, and in the debates of 1792 he proposed the immediate abolition of slavery. His action in English and Irish parliaments alike, during this period, shows him to have been both enlightened and independent; but with the progress of the French Revolution his division from the Foxites became marked. He was an enemy to Parliamentary Reform, and spoke against the motion of the future Lord Grey on May 7, 1793. His opinions were biassed by his fears of the Revolution, as his arguments show, and when these fears were past it was his lot to be a member of the Government which, under his old opponent, carried the Reform Bill of 1832. In 1790 he had travelled abroad for his health, and had seen in Paris the vagaries and violence which already marked the proceedings alike of the people and of the Assembly. In a letter to William Grenville[1] he gives an acute and humorous description of the state of the city, and it is not difficult to see how his experiences affected his opinions.

Lord Mornington's position was that of many young men of his time. He had no sympathy with narrow and antiquated Whiggism: he took a wide view of foreign politics and was keenly interested in philanthropic movements: he was greatly attached to the old Constitution, though not blind to its need of

---

[1] Dropmore MSS., vol. i. pp. 607-10.

reform: he was, in fact, in many ways a typical representative of the Conservatism which owed its birth to Pitt and to Burke. These principles appear clearly in a lengthy speech on the French Revolution, delivered on January 21, 1794, which he corrected for the press and published as a pamphlet, and to which Sheridan made and also published a vigorous reply. It is no slight testimony to the position he had won for himself that his speeches were generally answered by the greatest orators of the day. He did not always get the best of the encounter: of one famous debate Wilberforce wrote in his diary, 'Poor Mornington nervous and Sheridan brutal.'

In 1793 Lord Mornington was sworn of the English Privy Council, and in the same year he began his connection with Indian affairs by his appointment as a member of the Board of Control. He had already prepared himself by reading Indian history and such literature as he could procure[1]. For the next four years he studied India closely; his speeches contain constant allusions to the condition and policy of England in the East: and he had the advantage of an intimate acquaintance with Lord Cornwallis, whose Indian administration had been the most successful portion of his chequered career. His brother Arthur went out to Madras in 1796, with the character from

[1] He wrote from Brighton to Grenville, July 30, 1786, telling him that he was reading Orme, and asking for 'some general account of the European settlements in the East Indies.' Dropmore MSS., vol. i. p. 263.

Cornwallis of 'a sensible man and a good officer,' and from him he received constant communications, terse, acute, unprejudiced, like his later and more famous letters.

In the same year the necessity of changes in Indian administration became evident. Sir John Shore at Calcutta and Lord Hobart at Madras were impatient of each other's views. The latter expected to be made Governor-General; but the Home Government were convinced of his unfitness. Cornwallis was induced again to undertake the post, and in March 1797 Mornington was privately offered the Governorship of Fort St. George, with promise of the reversion of the Governor-Generalship. He accepted it, and it was not long before the reversion also fell to him.

On July 26, at the King's Levée he took leave, as for Madras; but the changes in Ireland were so great that it was felt Cornwallis could not be dispensed with. After a week at Holwood with Pitt, spent in anxious discussions of the needs and prospects of our Indian possessions, Mornington was definitely appointed Governor-General of India, receiving at the same time, as Baron Wellesley, a peerage of Great Britain, an honour he had long desired. At the end of October he took part in a great banquet given by the East India Company to the victor of Camperdown, and a ballad on the triumph of the great-hearted British Admiral, which he wrote for the occasion—not equal it must be confessed to those which Dibdin and Braham made so famous—was received with the enthusiasm which is generally the lot of a Viceroy's essays in verse. He was indeed better at Latin than at English poetry, and some hexameters on the crimes of the Revolution and the virtues of the venerable Duncan, written about the same time at Walmer and published in the Anti-Jacobin, were more worthy of his powers.

Lord Mornington sailed on November 7, 1797. From the first he affected all the dignities that should belong to the ruler of a great empire. Years before, on his first appearance in the Irish House of Lords, his *bel air* had been quizzed, and an ill-natured observer had compared his manner to that of Garrick as a tragedy-king. He had cultivated, indeed, all the outward graces of a great man: in attitude, in voice, in style, in the deliberation which had marked all his parliamentary utterances, he appeared as one who had a right to attention and homage. In lesser matters he was equally punctilious. On his way out, in spite of the distresses of a bad sailor [1], which he endured with much lamentation, he dressed for dinner as if he were at home; and the *Morning Chronicle*, in its account of his departure, reported with undisguised sarcasm, 'to such an extent is the frigate encumbered with stores, carriages, and baggage, that should the rencontre of an enemy make it necessary to prepare for action, Lord Mornington will inevitably suffer from clearage in the course of five minutes a loss of at least £2,000.'

[1] Even the crossing to Ireland made him ill enough to keep his bed. Dropmore MSS., vol. i. p. 225.

The new Governor-General went out, unlike some of his predecessors, pledged to no system and with practically no personal interest in the affairs which he was to direct. His brother Arthur was, it is true, already in India; and he took with him his youngest brother, Henry, as his political secretary. He was always eager to advance his kinsfolk, and his brothers more than justified his interest. But with this exception he was free from the slightest suspicion of concern outside the sphere of the duties of his post. Neither himself, nor through any agent, however well concealed, was he concerned in commerce. He had not, like Cornwallis, a military training or a military bias. No doubt he was influenced—most men were— by Dundas, but he was in no sense his creature. He had no past ties to the Company, and was neither indebted to them for his advancement nor relying upon them for future support. It was, too, a great advantage to come after such a man as Sir John Shore. Stolid and opinionated honesty is not generally attractive or engaging. Mornington's public life, while honourable to the core, was unquestionably a brilliant antithesis to that of his predecessor. He had much of the genius of Warren Hastings, and he started unhampered by ignorant opposition. Shore did better on a less extended area: of Mornington his friend the Speaker Addington, some years before, had said very truly, 'You want a wider sphere; you are dying of the cramp.'

CHAPTER II

BEGINNINGS IN INDIA: THE NIZÁM; THE PRESIDENCIES

AFTER the works of Sir James Stephen and Sir John Strachey[1] it would be idle again to insist upon the arbitrary and unhistorical dogmatism of James Mill. Be it only said that he is as hasty and pragmatical on Mornington as he is on Hastings, and as wilfully blind to the evidence which he professes to have consulted. The new Governor-General, he says, 'had possessed but little time for acquainting himself with the complicated affairs of India, when all his attention was directed to a particular point.' Were the time brief or long, the despatches which he wrote from the Cape of Good Hope on February 23 and February 28, 1798[2], show how well he had used it. It happened that he met at the Cape not only Lord Macartney, the Governor, who had been Governor of Madras, but also Lord Hobart, David Baird, who had been released from captivity in Mysore by the peace of Bangalore and had the best means of judging what were Tipú's

---

[1] *Nuncomar and Impey* (1885), and *Hastings and the Rohilla War* (1892).
[2] *Wellesley Despatches*, ed. Montgomery Martin, vol. i. pp. 1-15, 17-34.

feelings towards the English, and Major Kirkpatrick, who had recently been resident at Haidarábád. From the last-named he obtained information which Dundas especially desired as to the system 'now pursued almost universally by the native princes, of retaining in their service numbers of European or American officers under whom the native troops are trained and disciplined in imitation of the corps of Sepoys in the British service.' It was to this, and especially in regard to the relations of the Nizám with the Company, that Mornington on his arrival in India first directed his attention.

The Nizám's force, under the command of a Frenchman named Raymond, consisted of over ten thousand men with a train of about thirty native-served field-pieces. Orders had already been given for its increase to fourteen thousand: a large tract of country, part of which bordered on the Karnátik, had been assigned as security for its pay: and it was more than suspected, as it was afterwards proved, that the officers, with the tacit sanction of the Nizám himself, were in correspondence in the French interest with the far more dangerous ruler of Mysore. The position of this force was paralleled in many other native states, and it appeared to be clearly a distinct and powerful aid to French influence in India.

'I have no doubt,' wrote Mornington[1], 'that the natural effect of the unchecked and rapid growth of such a party at

[1] *Wellesley Despatches*, vol. i. p. 5.

the Court of one of our principal allies must be in a very short period to detach that Court entirely from our interests, and finally to fix it in those of our enemies; to subject its councils to their control, and its military establishments to their discretion. However despicable the corps of Raymond may now be in point of discipline or effect in the field, would it be wise to have such a large body of men in readiness to receive whatever improvements the ability, assiduity, and zeal of French officers sent from Europe for that express purpose might introduce into the constitution of a corps so prepared by correspondent principles and objects to meet the most sanguine expectations of their new leaders? Under these circumstances, the corps which perhaps now has little more efficiency than that of a political party, might soon become in the hands of our enemy as efficient a military force, as it is now in that view wholly useless either to the Nizám or to us.'

The measures by which Mornington, on the advice of Kirkpatrick, proposed to meet these dangers, were sketched thus early: and they were those which he actually carried out. They were—to procure by representation and demand the disbandment of Raymond's troops and to replace them by a large increase of the British contingent in the Nizám's pay, granting such extension of power in the use of the latter force as would enable it to be a real safeguard to the Nizám against the encroachments of the Maráthás. He discussed further, in his letter of the 23rd and at greater length on the 28th, the position of the British power in India in relation to the native states generally, and showed a masterly grasp of the situation and an intimate acquaintance with its difficulties which proved him to be no novice in the study of Indian politics. That his views were not merely derived from Kirkpatrick is clear from his discussion and rejection of several of that officer's proposals. It was to Haidarábád that Mornington first looked on his arrival in India. It will be convenient therefore to sketch his relations with the Nizám before we turn to the other branches of his work.

The position of the Nizám was, at this time, chiefly dangerous to the British because of his neighbourhood to and suspected dealings with the redoubtable ruler of Mysore. Tipú Sultán was the enemy whom the province of Madras had chiefly to fear, and his was the power which Mornington saw that it was necessary at once to reduce. But the Council of Fort St. George, shortsighted and timorous, remembered Haidar Alí's famous descent on the Karnátik and dreaded a war with his fierce and brutal son. They still fancied too, with singular blindness, that it was wise to suffer the extension of his power as a counterpoise to that of the Maráthás.

Mornington, it will be seen, had already proof of the hostile designs of Tipú, which made it madness to delay. He knew Mysore to be in alliance with France. Haidarábád, dominated by French officers, was certain sooner or later to follow the example. It was necessary, then, to act at once. Captain James Achilles Kirkpatrick was accordingly instructed to negotiate with the Nizám and with his son, Azím-al

Omrah, for a more definite and binding treaty. The details of the negotiation are to be gleaned chiefly in private correspondence[1]: but the action was prompt and effectual. Wellesley showed that he possessed not only the statesman's power of bold origination, but the skill, equally rare as it is, of choosing agents bold and decided as himself. Foremost among these was a young officer named Malcolm, of whose wide knowledge of the native languages and extensive study of the political systems of India he had learnt through his brother Henry Wellesley. Malcolm was appointed assistant at Haidarábád in September, 1798. His tact and courage were of the greatest service, and his subsequent brilliant career justified the selection. He became the historian of events in which he had been a prominent actor.

On September 1, 1798, a treaty was signed at Haidarábád by which the Nizám was to receive a subsidiary force of six thousand Sepoys with artillery officered by British subjects, to be paid out of his treasury. The whole of the officers and serjeants of the French force were to be dismissed ' and the troops composing it so dispersed and disorganized that no trace of the former establishment' should remain. No Frenchman was in future to be employed by the Nizám, nor any other European without the Company's permission.

Such was the treaty. To carry it out might seem

[1] The Sixth Report of the Royal Commission on Historical MSS. (Sir E. Strachey's MSS.) contains several letters from the Kirkpatricks.

a difficult matter. But Wellesley's agents were equal to the task imposed on them. It may be that if Raymond had been alive there would have been a fight: but he was dead and his successor, M. Perron, seems to have been glad to be out of the business. However that may be, through the tact and decision of Colonel Roberts, the disarmament of the French force was accomplished without difficulty, and British influence became once more supreme at Haidarábád. Thus, on the eve of the war with Tipú, which might prove the most serious that the Company had ever engaged in, the flank of the Madras presidency was secured, and what had been a danger was turned into a support.

To complete the record of Wellesley's relations with Haidarábád, it should be added that the Nizám took a subordinate part in the campaign in Mysore and received a very handsome share of the conquered territory. Before long a new treaty became necessary. The Nizám was in sore straits. The Maráthás, his constant and lively foes, were still pressing their claims for *chauth*: his own tributaries, who owed tribute also to the Maráthás, were encouraged by them in resistance to his demands. He could not coerce them, for his own force was inadequate and the British troops were, by treaty, only to be used for definite external war. The difficulties in the way of procuring an European-officered army were enormous. There seemed every possibility that before long the Maráthás would actually invade Haidarábád—and, last straw of all, the Nizám could exact no money from the territory he had gained in the Mysore partition, and his subsidy to the English was in arrears.

Under these circumstances a treaty of Defensive Alliance was negotiated in October 1800, by which Wellesley set at rest the difficulties of Haidarábád. The English forces in the Deccan were increased to ten thousand men, and were authorised to defend the Nizám against all aggression. The Nizám agreed to submit all his disputes to English mediation; and he yielded to the Company the whole of his acquisitions from Tipú. The northern frontier of Mysore was now placed in British hands, and the security of the Southern Province was greatly increased.

The disbandment of the French force, the earliest triumph of the new Governor-General, was cordially approved at home.

'Your treaty with the Nizám,' wrote Dundas, 'effectually puts an end to every alarm upon that part of the business; and whether you consider it negatively as removing the French force from our neighbourhood, or positively in respect of the additional strength it affords to us and the aid it gives to our finances, it is a transaction which tells in our favour in a variety of ways.... Your lordship has long before this time anticipated the satisfaction I have received from that transaction, which has been completed in so masterly and effectual a manner.'

In the course of his action with regard to the Nizám the Governor-General was brought into constant communication with the Governor and Council of Fort

St. George. The difficulties of control had always been one of the most fruitful sources of weakness in the Company's government of its possessions, and the situation during the time of Lord Hobart and Sir John Shore had become acute. To Mornington divided responsibility was intolerable, and he took the opportunity of the arrival of the new Governor of Madras, Lord Clive, to address to him a homily on his position and duties which is highly instructive. The tone is polite, cordial, friendly: Mornington received the intelligence of the appointment with 'very great pleasure'; but he did not hesitate to speak clearly. He emphasized the need for secrecy in communication: he criticized the inferiority of the civil service of Madras: he laid down strict limits as to the interference of the lesser with the greater official. No steps, he declared, must be taken in matters relating to negotiation, war, revenue, or the general interest, civil, military, or political of the Company's possessions, by the inferior presidency. Its duty consists merely 'in a cordial co-operation in the execution of that which it is the peculiar province of the Governor-General in Council to determine.' Nor is it compatible with the position of the lesser presidencies 'to mingle direct or indirect censures with their formal obedience to the legal authority of the Governor-General in Council; still less can it be their duty to anticipate his decisions by the premature interposition of their opinions or advice in any quarter, where such interference may counteract the success of his general plans and may introduce all the mischief and confusion of divided councils and of conflicting authority. The examination of the records of the late Government of Fort St. George,' continued the imperious Governor-General, ' will manifest a constant tendency towards this fatal error; and even since my arrival in Bengal I have found it necessary to restrain the symptoms of the same disposition.'

It was well to speak thus clearly at the outset; and it must be allowed that Lord Clive acted with great tact and restraint within the limits which his superior assigned to him. He refrained from the ·fatal error' of criticism, and the Governor-General went his lordly way, untrammelled by opposition, and followed to the end of his career by the 'fervent esteem, respect and affection[1]' of the subordinate whom he had taught thus early to know his place.

Difficulties there were with the Madras Council, where, especially in the case of the affairs of the Nawáb of Arcot, the officials were apt to act, as Arthur Young said that statesmen at home acted towards America, ' on the maxims of the counter'; but they were smoothed by the genuine friendship between Wellesley and Clive. Nor at any time did the condition of Madras approach that of Bombay. Of the latter, during his brother's administration

---

[1] See Lord Clive's letter on resigning his post to Lord William Bentinck, Sept. 3, 1803. *Wellesley Despatches*, vol. v. pp. 432-5.

(in spite of pleasant experience and a love passage [1]) Arthur Wellesley left a biting description which may sufficiently describe his relations with its Council:—

'There are two parties throughout the Bombay establishment, the civil and military service; and the latter are divided into two parties, those in the King's and those in the Company's service. The disputes of these two parties are the sole business of every man under the government of Bombay; and they are maintained by the system of encouragement given to correspondence and the perpetual reference to individuals by government. In short, I see that nothing can succeed with these people as it ought; and I wish to God I had nothing to do with them [2].'

[1] See *Bombay and Western India*, by James Douglas, vol. ii. p. 9.
[2] Nov. 11, 1803. Owen's *Selections from Wellington Despatches*, p. 320.

CHAPTER III

THE CONQUEST OF MYSORE

IN the popular mind the fame of Wellesley rested, and still rests, without question almost solely on the Conquest of Mysore. If the natives, as grotesque instances showed[1], regarded the Company as an old woman (a hypothesis to which its conduct gave a high degree of probability), the British nation, equally ignorant, knew the Indian States without discrimination as notable for wealth and cruelty, and the great peninsula as a happy land where the Company had sent Englishmen, and Mr. Dundas had sent Scotsmen, who returned after many years with impaired constitutions and impetuous manners to buy English constituencies and excite the avarice of poor relations. For once an Oriental chieftain came within the range of European politics. Whether because he was understood to be in alliance with the French bugbear or because so many Britons had been his prisoners, the barbarity of Tipú was a household word in England. Tipú was a sort of Eastern 'Boney'; English mothers

[1] Lord Valentia was announced to Wellesley thus—'The Lord's sister's son and the grandson of Mrs. Company is arrived.' See Torrens, *Wellesley*, p. 230.

scared their naughty children with his name. Colonel Wilks's account of the sufferings of British prisoners in Mysore[1] gives a picture which many a British household knew to be too sadly true. When General Baird's mother heard how the captives were bound together and dragged after the cannon on the march—'I pity the mon,' she said, 'wha's tied to ma Davie!' Few could treat the matter so lightly. Knowledge of the misery of the British prisoners led to exaggerated ideas of the power of the monster who had poisoned and assassinated so many of them. Haidar Alí had defeated the Company's troops in the open field: Tipú had stood forth with all the appearance of a conqueror at the peace of Mangalore in 1784, and in the fifteen years since then his power had seemed—in spite of his defeat at the hands of Cornwallis—rather to increase than to decay. Suddenly, in a few months, it was shattered to the dust; his territory was divided, his dynasty deposed; and the British troops secured such a quantity of prize-money as had never been known before. The British imagination, already strongly appealed to, was dazzled by these brilliant results; and when men at home asked whose work this was, and Anglo-Indians, military and civil servants alike, cried with one voice, 'Mornington's,' a testimony so unanimous and unusual carried all England with it in its enthusiasm. Wellesley, Tipú, and Seringapatam were written in the memories of

---

[1] *Historical Sketches of Southern India*, ii. 521, 2.

Englishmen for generations and in English history for all time.

Mornington[1] arrived in India with no settled plan of a Mysorean war. His instructions from Dundas were to preserve the balance of power between the native princes upon the same footing as that on which it was placed by the treaty of Seringapatam (1792). He perceived, from the conversations which he had at the Cape, and from the despatches from India which he opened and read, that this balance had been materially disturbed. The unsettled condition of the Marátha States was not such as to inspire alarm. The youth of Daulat Ráo Sindhia counterbalanced the accession of power which his predecessor, the great Mahadáji, had won. Indore was weakened by the feuds of the claimants to the authority of Túkají Holkar. Nágpur seemed to be stronger: but it was traditionally allied with the British. The Nizám was perceptibly weaker than of old. There was no power in Central or Southern India to be named beside that of Mysore. In the North-West Provinces the weakness of Oudh was a danger to the English and to itself; and there was an universal expectation of invasion from Zemán Sháh, the Afghán chief whose power had advanced with such alarming strides, and who was known to be in treaty with all the states in Hindustán that were unfriendly to the Company. It

---

[1] Besides the *Wellesley Despatches* there are on this subject *Select Letters of Tipú Sultán*, arranged and translated by Col. W. Kirkpatrick, 1811.

may be that this danger was exaggerated; but it is unquestionable that it appeared very real to all the prominent soldiers and statesmen of British India. Not the least alarming feature was the association of Zemán Sháh with Tipú Sultán.

Mornington sketched thus clearly, in his letter to Dundas from the Cape, the change in the position of the latter since the peace of Seringapatam.

'Since that period of time he has enjoyed perfect internal tranquillity; while our allies all around him have been distracted and exhausted by domestic rebellions, successive revolutions, and mutual wars, he has been employed in recruiting the sources of his strength, improving his revenues, and invigorating the discipline of his armies.... He has been very active for some time past in his application to the Courts of the Native powers, endeavouring to stir them up against us. He certainly applied for that purpose to the Nizám, and during the absence of Azím ul Omrah at Poona he made a very strong impression upon the politics of the Court of Haidarábád, where he has now a *vakíl*, and where he certainly has many partisans as well in the corps of Raymond as in the service of Umjid ul Daula, a chief of a considerable faction called the Paungah party, and in that of Imtiaz ul Daula, nephew to the Nizám. Tipú has also sent *vakíls* to Poona, with the same object of raising a spirit of hostility against us.'

After discussing the policy to be adopted towards the other States, he continues:

'I have adverted in this letter to the increased assiduity with which Tipú has endeavoured to raise animosities against us among the Native powers, and to his intercourse with

Zemán Shâh. I wish to know from you whether we ought to suffer without animadversion and spirited representation such open acts of hostility on the part of Tipú ? My ideas on this subject are that, as on the one hand we ought never to use any high language towards Tipú, nor ever attempt to deny him the smallest point of his machinations against us, we ought to let him know that his treachery does not escape our observation, and to make him feel that he is within the reach of our vigilance. At present it appears to me that he is permitted to excite ill-will against us wherever he pleases, without the least attempt on our part to reprehend either him for the suggestion, or the court to whom he applies for listening to it.'

Moderation, however, was impossible when Tipú's relations with the French became known. He had for some time (as it was afterwards discovered by the papers found at Seringapatam) been corresponding with the French governor of Mauritius, giving him information of the state of India and pressing for an immediate invasion. It was not till the correspondence had continued for some time, and Tipú had sent envoys to negotiate by word of mouth, that the Governor of Mauritius definitely accepted the offers of the ruler of Mysore.

On June 8 Mornington read in a Calcutta newspaper the proclamation issued by Governor Malartie in January. The proclamation stated the requests of Tipú for assistance and his promises of service against the English. He had declared that all his preparations were already completed, and that the French troops, whom he would maintain entirely at his own expense, would find everything ready for immediate war; that, in fact, he only waited for French succour to open hostilities against the English, and that it was his ardent desire to expel them from India. On the ground of these statements the proclamation recommended a general levy for the service, and assured all citizens who should enlist that Tipú would give them a good rate of pay and allowances, to be fixed by his envoys before the departure of the expedition.

Mornington at once began to make preparations for war. He wrote immediately to General Harris at Madras, warning him to make preparations. Advice poured in upon him from the timid officials at Madras. Most characteristic was the memorandum of Mr. Josiah Webbe, the honest and able Secretary to that Presidency. He dwelt upon the 'principle of British policy,' to preserve Tipú as a power and to balance him against the Maráthás and the Nizám, upon the military weakness, the lack of resources, the bankruptcy of the Madras presidency, the strength of Tipú's defences, and the utter weakness of our allies. 'I can anticipate none but the most baneful consequences from a war with Tipú.'

So said they all. Even General Harris dwelt strongly on the difficulties in the way. Nor was Mornington himself blind to the want of allies. No aid, he said, could be expected from the Nizám, weakened by his long wars with the Maráthás, or from Poona, where dissensions and Sindhia alike prevented any active interference, and where the one constant principle was hatred of Haidarábád. Happily, support was not lacking from home. The Secret Committee wrote, as soon as they heard of the proclamation, to direct that, if Tipú's designs should prove to be such as that document represented, his attack should not be awaited, but war should at once be carried into the enemy's country. Mornington received this letter on October 18, and he heard at the same time of Bonaparte's Egyptian expedition. It was clear that no time was to be lost. He issued orders to the Madras authorities to prepare for war, and pressed on the disarmament of the French troops at Haidarábád. His letters show a thorough grasp of the objects to be sought and of the means to be used: he appears to have mastered detail and principle alike. The long minute of August 12, 1798, written for the Council and occupying fifty pages of the despatches, is a work of consummate genius, and by itself would establish its author's claim to be a statesman of the highest rank. His objects were thus summarised:

'First, to seize the whole maritime territory remaining in his possession below the Gháts on the coast of Malabar, in order to preclude him from all future communications by sea with his French allies. Secondly, by marching the army from the coast of Coromandel directly upon his capital, to compel him to purchase peace by a formal cession of the territory seized on the coast of Malabar. Thirdly, to compel him to defray our whole expense in the war, and thus to secure the double advantage of indemnifying us for the expense occasioned by his aggression, and of reducing his resources with a view to our future security. Fourthly, to compel him to admit permanent Residents at his Court from us and from our allies, a measure which would enable us at all times to check his operations, and to counteract the intricacies of his treachery. Fifthly, that the expulsion of all the natives of France now in his service, and the perpetual exclusion of all Frenchmen, both from his army and dominions, should be made conditions of any treaty of peace with him.'

His opinions clear, his measures decided, he advanced rapidly towards his end. On November 4 he conveyed to Tipú intelligence of the British success in Egypt; on the 8th, still hoping to prevent a rupture, he urged him in a dignified letter to abandon the French alliance. On Christmas Day, 1798, he received a shuffling reply, attributing to the French the spreading of false reports, and ending in the true Oriental diplomatic vein:

'Your lordship is a great Sirdar, a firm friend and the rectifier of all things, and you possess an enlightened judgement. I have the strongest hope that the minds of the wise and intelligent will not be sullied by doubts and jealousies, but will consider me from my heart desirous of harmony and friendship. Continue to allow me the pleasure of your correspondence, making me happy by accounts of your health. What more shall be written!'

Mornington advanced towards his end with sure and certain tread. On the very day he received this insolent letter he sailed for Madras. He arrived on December 31, and on January 2, 1799, assumed the direction of affairs at the scene of action. On the

9th he wrote a clear and determined letter to Tipú, explaining that he knew of his negotiations with the French, and calling upon him definitely to receive an English envoy and make terms with the Company and its allies. No satisfactory reply was sent: no news had arrived of the ultimate fortune of the French in Egypt. The danger was pressing. A letter from the Sultán of Turkey himself, the head of the Muhammadan interest, desiring him to ally with the British, left Tipú still unwilling to surrender his hopes from the French alliance. He only replied to Mornington that he was going a-hunting. His cup was full. Mornington delayed no longer.

There can be no question that the judgement of the Company's officials as to the growth of the power of Tipú and the decay of the other states was just: still less can the reality of the French intrigues be doubted. Two further points, however, on which Mr. Mill lays great stress, must be considered. Was Wellesley precipitate in the declaration of war? The long period during which plans were laid and preparations matured, long indeed in comparison with that which precedes the wars of our own day, appears to refute this charge. It must be remembered also that delay was in every way favourable to Tipú. It made his chances of French help stronger and gave him time to strengthen his defences. If it was necessary to strike at all, certainly it was wise to strike soon.

But there is a more serious charge. Tipú, it is declared, was a man of religion and moderation :—

'As a domestic ruler he sustains an advantageous comparison with the greatest prince of the East. . . . He had the discernment to perceive, what is generally hid from the eyes of rulers in a more enlightened state of society, that it is the prosperity of those who labour with their hands which constitutes the principle and cause of the prosperity of States; he therefore made it his business to protect them against the intermediate orders of the community, by whom it is difficult to prevent them from being oppressed. His country was accordingly, at least during the first and better part of his reign, the best cultivated, and its population the most flourishing in India; while under the English and their dependents, the population of the Karnátik and Oudh, hastening towards the state of deserts, was the most wretched upon the face of the earth [1].'

A comparison with States in which the Company had at that moment no authority or power of reform is, to say the least, disingenuous; and it need only be replied that the testimony of residents and travellers far from bears out the Utopian description of Mr. Mill. The increased prosperity of the country under British rule is vouched for by indisputable authority. And it would be difficult to say what foundation in fact is possessed by Mr. Mill's application to the Sultán of Mysore of his own excellent sentiments concerning the position of the agricultural labourer. The taxation under Tipú was oppressive, and the sons of the soil paid heavily for tilling it.

So much of preliminaries and justification. On February 22, 1799, Mornington issued at Madras

[1] Mill, *History of British India*, ed. Wilson, vol. vi. pp. 105, 6.

a declaration of the occasions of the war, and on the same day sent to General Harris his instructions for the political conduct of the campaign. These chiefly concerned the appointment of a Commission, of which Arthur Wellesley was to be the head, to negotiate with any tributaries or subjects of Tipú who might desire to ally with the British, and to use measures of conciliation towards the inhabitants of the invaded territory, and of protection to any surviving member of the old ruling family of Mysore dispossessed by the adventurer Haidar.

In a private letter to General Harris, Mornington expressed himself happy in the advantageous circumstances under which the war was to be begun. The army of the Karnátik, which Harris was to command, was unquestionably 'the best appointed, the most completely equipped, the most amply and liberally supplied, the most perfect in point of discipline, and the most fortunate in the acknowledged experience and abilities of its officers in every department, which ever took the field in India.' The army on the Malabar coast was equally efficient. Both were strong in cavalry: and Wellesley now expected, somewhat too sanguinely, some results from the zeal displayed by the Nizám, and the aid of a not inconsiderable detachment of the famed Marátha horse. Harris was to go unshackled by the civil control which had spoiled so many a British expedition in the past. The object of the war was 'single, distinct, and definite,' and the means of attaining it had long been studied by those to whom it was entrusted to carry them out. The whole of the British staff was well acquainted with the geography, the resources and the defences of Mysore.

'On the other hand, Tipú's army is known to have suffered considerably both in numbers and discipline since the last war. His finances are in great disorder; he no longer possesses the confidence of his army, his counsels are distracted by a variety of contending factions, and his spirits are dejected and broken by the disappointment of his hopes of French assistance, by the retreat of Zemán Sháh, by the failure of his intrigues at the Courts of Poona and Haidarábád, and by the unexampled vigour, alacrity, and extent of our military operations.'

A glowing picture—the colours bright to encourage the cautious soldier. Mornington knew how to sound a trumpet call to action as well as how to pen a diplomatic protocol or a statesman's estimate of political probabilities. Once more he addressed the Court of Directors in a dignified vindication of the war. Already he had ordered the army to advance.

On the day that the formal act of opening the war took place, the Governor-General wrote a letter to Colonel Palmer, the Resident at Poona, which expresses with brevity and clearness the aims which he held at the moment.

'Entertaining no views of aggrandisement, my objects in the war will be limited to the attainment of a just indemnity for the great expense to which the aggression of Tipú Sultán has subjected the allies, and of a reasonable security against the future violence and treachery of that prince. But no negotiations with a view to either object can be entertained without danger to the common cause until the Sultán shall have been compelled to entertain serious apprehension for the security of Seringapatam. And it is accordingly my resolution to listen to no overtures from him until we shall have attained such a position as shall sufficiently secure us against the efforts of his insincerity. In this determination I have no doubt of being cordially supported by the Peshwá and by Nána Farnavis[1].'

On February 3, General Harris took the command; on March 5, his troops entered the territory of Mysore. A Bombay contingent under General Stewart advanced to form a junction with the Madras army. The march was no military promenade, nor was it accomplished with the order which befits a well organized force. The difficulty of keeping open communications was considerable, that of transport was greater, that of obtaining supplies greater still. Stewart advanced by the Poodicherran Ghát and stationed his army between Sídasíre and Sidapore, where he was attacked by Tipú, whom he repelled with considerable slaughter. The united forces of Madras and Bombay then advanced by Kánkánhalli; while Tipú, who had retired to Seringapatam after his defeat, again came forward, but with hesitating and uncertain plan. Finally he gave battle at Malvilli. The fight was sharp, and not without vigour on the part of the Mysorean army; but it ended in another victory for the British troops,

---

[1] Feb. 3, 1799. *Selections from Letters, &c.* at Bombay, by G. W. Forrest, Maráthá Series, vol. i.

and Tipú retired again to his capital. This was on March 27: on April 5, General Harris completed the investment and began the siege. The operations were hurried as much as possible, for the season was late and want of supplies was already being felt. Nor were the forts behind the invaders secured. It had been a bold rush and everything was staked on the rapidity of the movements.

On the evening of April 3, the breach made by the artillery in the walls was considered practicable, and on the 4th the assault took place under the command of Major-General Baird. 'In less than seven minutes from the period of issuing from the trenches the British colours were planted on the summit of the breach.' Within the ramparts there was fierce resistance. Tipú himself was in the thick of the fight and fell, covered with wounds, as the British entered the inner fortification [1]. The triumph was complete.

Baird, who commanded the attack, had himself undergone cruel imprisonment at Tipú's hands, and was not remarkable for lenity: but his treatment of the Sultán's children was generous and noble. When he saw the princes trembling and distressed he was, says an eye-witness [2], 'sensibly affected ... and his gallantry on the assault was not more conspicuous

---

[1] An interesting account of Tipú's conduct during the siege and on his last day is to be found in the *Persian Life* by Mír Hussein Alí Khán, translated by Col. Miles, London, 1844. The Sultán is regarded as a hero and martyr.

[2] Major Allan, in Beatson's *View of the War with Tipú Sultán*, Appendix xlii.

than the moderation and humanity which on this occasion he displayed. He received the princes with every mark of regard, repeatedly assured them that no violence or insult should be offered to them, and he gave them in charge to two officers to conduct them to head-quarters in camp.'

With Tipú's death the war was practically at an end: the fortresses of Mysore speedily surrendered, the people apparently welcomed the change of masters: only a predatory adventurer, named Dhundia Wágh, kept up a guerilla warfare for some time till he was defeated and slain by Arthur Wellesley.

In the settlement of Mysore the objects of the Governor-General were twofold. It was essential to obtain reasonable indemnification for the cost of the war and to secure Madras against the recurrence of a danger so great as had been associated with the growth of the Muhammadan State in the south. The task of redistribution of territory and power was a difficult one. The Nizám and the Maráthás must be rewarded for their support. The former had given aid of some value and he looked for the lion's share of the spoil. But to have given him an equal proportion of the conquered territory to that reserved for the Company would have aggrandised his power beyond the limits of discretion, and, moreover, have been a cause of great jealousy to the Maráthás. On the other hand, the Maráthás had not aided in the war; their attitude had been one of subservient inactivity; but, like jackals, they looked for a share in the game. Mornington observed with justice that all they might receive would be 'gratuitous on the part of the Company and the Nizám[1].' To have given them a share equal to that of the Nizám or the British would have been both impolitic and unjust.

Such divisions of the land as would have entirely satisfied either the Nizám or the Maráthás would have kept the British frontier still insecure. But Mornington saw that it would be equally imprudent to increase the Company's territories out of proportion to the gains of the native states. Accordingly, as he stated in his despatch to the Directors of August 3, 1799, he regulated the division on the following principles—'An attentive consideration of every comparative view of these important questions terminated in my decision that the establishment of a central and separate government in Mysore, under the protection of the Company, and the admission of the Maráthás to a certain participation in the division of the conquered territory, were the expedients best calculated to reconcile the interests of all parties, to secure the Company a less invidious and more efficient share of revenue, resource, commercial advantage and military strength than could be obtained under any other distribution of territory or power, and to afford the most favourable prospect of general and permanent tranquillity in India[2].' The

---

[1] Letter to Col. Palmer. Forrest's *Selections from Bombay Letters &c.*, Marátha Series, vol. i. p. 630.

[2] Despatches, vol. ii. p. 75.

following accordingly was the actual division of territory.

1. The English took the province of Kánara, the districts of Koimbatúr, Darapúram and Mujnad, with all the land below the Gháts, between Malabar and the Karnátik, securing an uninterrupted tract of territory from the coast of Coromandel to that of Malabar, together with the entire sea-coast of the kingdom of Mysore. Besides this, the fortress of Seringapatam and the forts commanding the heads of the passes above the Gháts were placed in British hands.

2. The Nizám obtained the districts of Gooty and Gurramkonda, and land down to Chitaldrúg and other border fortresses of Mysore.

3. To the Maráthás was assigned territory in value rather more than half that of the other powers: but on condition that the Peshwá should enter into definite agreement against the French and undertake never to employ Europeans without the Company's consent, and should guarantee the inviolability of the new State to be erected in Mysore. The Peshwá, with extraordinary blindness, refused the offer, and the territory which he declined was divided between the English and the Nizám.

4. The rest of Tipú's dominions, now surrounded east and west by the Company's territories and defended on the north by a strong line of fortresses, was given to the descendant of the old Hindú Rájás whom Haidar Alí had dispossessed. The establish-

ment of the Hindu Rájá was a politic concession to the feelings of the population by whom the Muhammadan rule had been hated as well as feared. But the subsidiary treaty of Seringapatam, signed on June 22, 1799, placed the government of the new Rájá entirely under British control, and gratitude as well as obligation attached him to the power which had raised him from obscurity.

The settlement was left in the hands of a Commission on which sat Mornington's brothers, Arthur, who had won considerable distinction in the war, and Henry. On the dissolution of the Commission, Colonel Close became British resident with the new Rájá, and Arthur Wellesley was placed in command of the troops left in the country.

Well might Mornington look with pride upon the results of his prompt and daring action. A year before he landed in India it would not have been thought possible for the Company to overthrow the power of Tipú. Through his determination the task had been accomplished with ease in two months. In his despatch to the Directors he stated the advantages obtained, in language through the sobriety of which appears a proud and dignified elation. An immediate addition of £259,000 per annum to their territorial revenue, which, with the increased payment from the Nizám and the profits to be expected from better cultivation of the soil, would soon, he estimated, amount to over £1,000,000 additional revenue: the Kárnátik placed in a complete position for defence;

the great increase of English commerce by the removal of the restrictions of Tipú; the improvement of the Company's army through increased supply-grounds and new fields for recruiting—these were some of the advantages which Mornington anticipated from his great conquest. But these were not all. 'Highly,' he continues, 'as I estimate these immediate and direct advantages of revenue and of commercial and military resources, I consider the recent settlement of Mysore to be equally important to your interests in its tendency to increase your political consideration and influence among the native powers of India, together with your means of maintaining internal tranquillity and order among your subjects and dependants, and of defending your possessions against any enemy either Asiatic or European.' And lastly, as the Governor-General foresaw, it was the final and complete overthrow of the French influence in India.

On the settlement of Mysore and its actual results a word may be necessary. The position of the Company was stronger in Mysore than in the other states which were about this period subjected to British control. 'Owing to the inconveniences and embarrassments arising,' says Mornington himself, 'from the system of double government and conflicting authorities in Oudh, the Karnátik, and Tanjore, I resolved to reserve to the Company the most extensive and indisputable powers.' The Rájá, as he was the creature, was the subject, of the British. The sovereignty was practically in the hands of the conquerors of Mysore.

The future justified to the fullest extent the wisdom of Mornington's action.

Arthur Wellesley wrote in 1801, 'The Rájá's government is in the most prosperous state: the country is becoming a garden, where it is inhabited, and the inhabitants are returning fast to those parts which the last savage had forced them to quit .... Mysore is become a large and handsome native town, full of inhabitants; the whole country is settled and in perfect tranquillity. I believe the Rájá's treasury is rich, as he pays his kists with regularity; but Poorneah (the chief minister of Tipú, continued by the English as Dewan), who has an eye to the future prosperity and revenue of the country, has repaired numberless tanks .... has rebuilt many towns and forts; and, I understand, encourages the inhabitants of the country in all parts by advances of money and remissions whenever they require them. Thus their establishment has succeeded in a manner equal to our most sanguine expectations, and there is every prospect that its prosperity will be permanent [1].' And in 1804, in an official letter to the Governor-General, he gave a more detailed description of the condition of the new State in terms as congratulatory [2]. And again, two years later, he could write [3]:—

'The state in which this government is to be found at this moment, the cordial and intimate union which exists between

---

[1] Owen, *Selections from the Wellington Despatches*, pp. 541-2.
[2] Ibid., 551 sqq.
[3] Owen, *Selections from the Wellesley Despatches*, p. lxxxii.

the Government of Mysore and the British authorities, and the important strength and real assistance which it has afforded to the British Government in all its recent difficulties, afford the strongest proof of the wisdom of the foundation on which those relations were laid [1].'

When the news of the fall of Seringapatam was made public the enthusiasm of the British settlements in India knew no bounds. Addresses of congratulation poured in upon the Governor-General, and, if he had allowed it, it would have 'rained' gifts. At a thronged meeting of the inhabitants of Madras, who had lived in fear of the great Muhammadan adventurers for twenty years, an address, grandiloquent in jubilation, was carried by enthusiastic acclamation:—

'A prudence less penetrating, or a vigour less active, might have been appalled,' says the eloquence of the enthusiastic merchants, 'at the difficulties of supporting a war against the kingdom of Mysore; but it was the peculiar energy of your lordship's mind, to anticipate the growth and maturity of those difficulties, to estimate the true extent of our own power, to seize the critical period of action, and to create resources, by inspiring a confidence and energy correspondent to the extent and importance of your lordship's measures. The result of those measures we now view with triumph and exultation, in the complete subversion of the power of Tipú Sultán, of whose enmity the determined inveteracy rendered peace undesirable; and whose infatuated attachment to the implacable enemy of England rendered war unavoidable. The rapidity with which this great event

[1] Memorandum on state of India, in Owen's *Selections from the Wellesley Despatches*, p. lxxxii.

has, under Providence, by your lordship's wisdom and the gallantry of the army, been achieved, has left on our minds an impression of admiration, at a conquest unequalled in its importance in the annals of British India. The brilliancy of this conquest has spread a blaze of glory over the meridian of your lordship's government; and from the extensive influence of its effects, we have a just confidence that your lordship's career in India will close by diffusing throughout Hindustán the calm of genuine peace and undisturbed tranquillity[1].'

No less eloquent was the homage of Bombay:—

'In the result of this conquest, as unprecedented in the rapidity of its completion. as it is unequalled in its importance, we behold the entire extinction of a cruel and relentless foe, a valuable acquisition of territory and power, the strength of our alliances in India increased, a destructive confederacy dissolved and defeated; which, whilst it affords us the fairest prospect of a permanent internal tranquillity and security, relieves us also from the apprehension of external violence and invasion, by giving us a well-grounded confidence, that it must effectually frustrate the machinations and intrigues of the Directory of France, the inveterate and implacable foe of England, and the common enemy of established order, liberty, and government, in every part of the world[2].'

Calcutta, no less exultant, declared in more measured strain that 'to your lordship's vigilance, energy, and wisdom Great Britain is indebted for all these great events.'

The Houses of Lords and Commons unanimously passed votes of thanks in the same terms, dwelling upon the wisdom, decision, and energy of the Governor-

---

[1] *Wellesley Despatches*, vol. i. pp. 621-2.   [2] Ibid., pp. 624-6.

General; and the East India Company, in tamer language, recognised the achievements of its servants.

Dearer still, it cannot be doubted, to the heart of Mornington, was the unstinted and remarkable homage of the Army. It is not often that to a civilian is attributed the entire credit of a great military success, or that soldiers are willing to share their honours with a man of peace. But Mornington inspired something of the feeling that was aroused by the commanding genius of Pitt. The Army presented him with the star and badge of the order of St. Patrick, made from the jewels of Tipú. General Harris, in sending the gift, wrote:—

'In performing this pleasing duty I am proud to feel and to acknowledge that the splendid success of the late campaign must, under divine Providence, be in justice referred to the instructive wisdom and characteristic energy of your Lordship's councils. Those councils have formed a memorable era in the history of India. From their effects the Company has gained a new source of increasing prosperity, and in their operation the wide-spread interests of the British Empire in the East, being consolidated and raised on a firm and durable basis, have attained an eminence of elevation and security hitherto unknown. The glory of having been made by your lordship instrumental to the acquirement of some of these inestimable advantages, excites in my mind feelings of satisfaction and gratitude which no language can adequately convey.'

The reception of the magnificent gift was characteristic. The Governor-General declined to receive the present, as precluded by the letter of the law; and when later Dundas wrote to tell him that an offer of £100,000 from the prize-money would be made him by the Company, he again declined the gift, refusing with magnanimous spirit to deprive the soldiers of any share in the profits of the great triumph. 'I should be miserable,' he said, 'if I could ever feel that I had been enriched at the expense of those who must ever be the objects of my affection, admiration, and gratitude, and who are justly entitled to the exclusive enjoyment of all that a munificent king and an admiring country can bestow.' The Directors expressed their approval of his action, but conferred on him an annuity of £5,000 for twenty years, and desired him to accept the jewels offered by the Army.

A reward which he prized far more highly was the almost unique honour conferred by the Crown in 1801, when he was made Captain-General and Commander-in-Chief of all the forces in the East Indies. This was a distinction which appealed to his strongest passion. He assumed all the ensigns of military authority. He loved to live at Barrackpur, surrounded by his soldiers, and planning, when occasion arose, those masterly movements which not a soldier in India could have designed with such foresight or such skill. The pomp and circumstance in which he delighted were now his to the full; the bodyguard on which he had set so much store was now his by a double title; and he was, and remained to the end of his rule, the idol of the brave troops whom it was his highest honour to command.

These were the rewards which he valued. But the

recognition of his services which he most desired was denied him. A dukedom, or at least an English peerage of high rank, was, he conceived, no more than his due. Pitt wrote to him that he was to be raised to an Irish marquisate, and said all the kind things that a friend would say. But Mornington, 'not having yet received,' as he said, 'my double-gilt potato,' sent a letter of bitter complaint in reply.

Much has been written about his egregious vanity and absurd self-appreciation—much that is beside the point. Whether the title he now obtained was not high enough for one whose period of service had been so short may be a fit question. Quite other was the aspect in which the matter must have appeared to the Governor-General himself. One step in the Irish peerage, from Earl of Mornington to Marquess of Wellesley, seemed but a very small reward. Among Pitt's lavish creation of peerages the services recognised had been mechanical and mediocre in comparison with such achievements as his. Successful merchants, sound voters, comfortable men of property, had been poured into the House of Lords. Wellesley had prevented the extension of the European war to an Asiatic battleground; he had destroyed the most dangerous power in India; he might feel that he had created an empire; and he received one step in the Irish peerage. His father had been raised from a Barony to an Earldom for services which it would have puzzled a herald to discover. The great Pro-Consul felt the irony, and could not conceal that he felt it.

CHAPTER IV

THE KARNÁTIK, TANJORE, OUDH

CHIEF among the tributary states of the British power in India stood the Karnátik. Here, from the infancy of the English settlements, there had been trouble and confusion, and as time went on the confusion became worse confounded. Previous volumes in this series have explained in detail the relations between the Company and the Nawáb. They may here be best summed up in the words of Sir Arthur Wellesley's Memorandum on the condition of India during his brother's rule, written in 1806 [1]:—

'The general purport of them at all times had been protection of the Karnátik by the Company, on the condition of the regular monthly payment of a stipulated subsidy by the Nawáb; that the Nawáb should have no political communication with any foreign power excepting through the intervention or with the consent of the Company; that the Company should not interfere in the internal concerns of the Nawáb's government; and that the last treaty of 1792 provided particularly that in case of failure in the payment of the stipulated subsidy certain countries should be ceded to the Company.'

This understanding had been violated in almost

---

[1] It is printed in Mr. Sidney Owen's admirable *Selections from the Wellesley Despatches*. The passage here quoted is on p. lxxxvi.

every particular. It was indeed impossible to maintain so anomalous an arrangement. The Company were not to interfere in the internal government of the Nawáb, but the state of the Karnátik was so rotten that interference was continually necessary. The subsidy was a burden which could only have been borne by economy and care in the management of the finances; but there was no economy and no management worthy the name. The Nawábs, pitiable in their abasement, were never out of the hands of the money-lenders. They borrowed from gentlemen in the Company's service, contrary to the express order of the Company, and that at the extortionate rate of three per cent. *per mensem*. In security for the payment of the interest the wretched Nawábs had been obliged to assign large tracts of land to their creditors, whom they appointed as collectors of revenue from the districts.

'Here then,' says Wellington, 'was established a system which tended not only to the oppression of the inhabitants of the country, to the impoverishment of the Nawáb and to the destruction of the revenues of the Karnátik, but it was carried into execution by the Company's civil and military servants, and by British subjects.' The evil was indeed even worse than is here represented; for a number of English gentlemen became interested, as the Nawáb's creditors, in the maintenance of this disgraceful condition of affairs. It had been ordered by the treaty of 1792 that no further assignment should be made on the districts which were pledged to the Company as security for the payment of the subsidy; but the Nawáb having less interest in the prosperity of these districts, since they were already pledged, than in any other part of his dominions, did not hesitate to assign them again, nor did the creditors demur, since they were among the richest of his lands.

Neither Cornwallis nor Shore had been able to remedy the evils, and the situation at the beginning of Lord Mornington's governorship was rendered more acute by the war with Tipú. On April 24, 1799, Mornington wrote to the Nawáb, pointing out that, war having been declared with Mysore, it became necessary, under the treaty of 1792, for the Company to assume the administration and collect the revenues of the Karnátik. He drew attention also to the breaches of the past treaties, and suggested heads for a new treaty by which certain districts should be placed under the exclusive control of the Company [1]. To this the Nawáb replied after some delay, on May 13, when he had heard of the capture of Seringapatam, in a manner designed to avoid any settlement of the difficulties. Happily, the capture of Seringapatam enabled Wellesley to put an end to the Nawáb's shuffling. Among the papers of Tipú were discovered letters from the Nawábs Muhammad Alí and Omdal ul Omrah to Haidar Alí and Tipú Sultán,

---

[1] India Office MSS. Miscellaneous Records, vol. xix, contains numerous letters (1799-1800) of the Nawáb to the Governor-General, to Dundas, and to Lord Clive, as to his debts and position, with protests on various points, particularly on vexatious acts of Lord Hobart's government.

which incontestably proved their treachery towards the British.

I say incontestably. But James Mill argues that no credit can be attached to the statements of the Nawáb's envoys to Tipú (who were examined), and that after all they stated nothing of importance; that the letters themselves prove nothing; and that the wolf will always find a justification for his slaughter of the lamb.

The Nawábs had more affinity to a black sheep than a guileless lamb, it may be replied. But the facts which Mill himself admits show the improbability of any foul play. A commission was appointed to examine the evidence, and the names of Mr. Webbe and Colonel Close were guarantees of integrity. 'Every precaution was taken,' says Mill, 'such as that of preventing communications between the witnesses, to get from them either the evidence pure or the means of detecting its impurity.' The foremost men in India, the Governor-General and Council, the Governor and Council of Madras, the Commissioners, and also Mr. Neil Edmonstone, the Persian interpreter—a most eminent civilian—did not doubt that the papers established treacherous relations between the Nawáb and Tipú. 'It is very remarkable,' says Mr. Mill. Remarkable indeed if their judgement was incorrect; and more remarkable still since it was confirmed by Dundas and the Secret Committee at home. Mornington's own despatch (of May 28, 1801) shows no tendency to exaggerate the weight of evidence, and it does not appear that the charge was ever seriously denied.

There was no precipitation in the enquiry. More than eighteen months elapsed between the discovery of the papers and the decision of the Governor-General. Wellesley could afford to wait for a final settlement. Before the time for this arrived, difficulties were smoothed by the death of Omdal ul Omrah on July 15, 1801. On May 28 Wellesley had written to Lord Clive [1], Governor of Madras, stating concisely the facts as to the treachery of the Nawábs and its investigation, and requesting him to inform Omdal ul Omrah that it would be necessary for the Company to assume the entire civil and military government of the Karnátik. He enclosed a terse mandate to the Nawáb to the same effect. Three days later, and again on June 4, Wellesley sent directions for the course to be pursued in the event of the death of the Nawáb, who was dangerously ill. The dispute as to the succession between Alí Husain, the reputed son of the late Nawáb, and his nephew, Azím u'd Daulah, made the settlement easier. The former having rejected the offer of the succession on the condition that he should assent to Wellesley's terms, the latter was established by treaty on July 31, 1801. On the 27th a declaration had been published in which Wellesley justified *urbi et orbi* the practical annexation of the Karnátik. The complete civil and military administration of the land was vested in the Company. One-fifth of the

---

[1] *Wellesley Despatches*, ii. 515 sqq.

net revenues was assigned to the Nawáb, and provision was made for the gradual liquidation by the Company of his registered debts.

The justice of this arrangement, no less than the personal action of Lord Wellesley, is impugned by Mr. Mill. His criticism depends entirely on the supposition that the Nawábs of the Karnátik were originally and had continued to be independent princes. This they had never been. They were merely officers of the Subahdar of the Deccan. Of him they had been rendered independent by the British, whose creatures they had therefore become. Wellesley, though even he appeared to recognise in them an independence to which they had no claim, treated them as subject-princes disloyal to the power to whom they owed obedience. Undoubtedly too much appearance of freedom had been allowed them by various governors; but this did not affect the legal position of the government when it came finally into question.

The result of the arrangement was security rather than annexation. Before it the Company had been charged with the defence of the Karnátik without the means of rendering it defensible. The frontier for which they now became responsible was not increased, but their power over the land became substantial where it had been insecure. The assumption of the real control by the British Government was followed by a considerable increase in the prosperity of the country as well as in the revenues which it produced[1].

[1] India Office MSS. No. 207, vol. 175, contains an account of the

Mornington on his arrival in India had to meet difficulties in Tanjore and Surat, and he met them in a manner similar to that of his treatment of the Karnátik. The affairs of Tanjore were, in the words of Dundas, 'more simple in their nature and less complicated in their administration' than those of Arcot. The question was one of succession. Had the halfbrother of the late Rájá, or his adopted son, the better right to the *masnad*? The former had acted as regent for the latter for many years, and the legal right had been referred to pandits for decision. The enquiry had terminated in favour of Sarbojí, the son, but there had been great delay in giving effect to it. Sarbojí had been commended by the late Rájá to the care of the Danish missionary Schwarz, and had grown up an able and cultivated man. Amír Singh, the uncle, had been guilty of truly Oriental misgovernment [1].

On November 26, 1799, a treaty with Sarbojí was ratified at Calcutta [2], which Wellesley briefly described in a letter to the Secret Committee two days later as 'investing the entire and exclusive administration,

management of the revenue of the Karnátik and of Tanjore in 1771-2 compared with 1801-2.

[1] 'A quarter of a century later he was portrayed by Bishop Heber as one of the most singularly gifted and accomplished persons he had ever known, being able to quote Lavoisier and Linnaeus fluently, to appreciate fine distinctions of character in Shakespeare, to write fair English verse, and withal to hold his own with cavalry officers in judging the points of a horse, or killing a tiger at long range.' Torrens, *Marquess Wellesley*, p. 205.

[2] *Wellesley Despatches*, vol. ii. App. A.

civil and military, of "Tanjore" in the Company's government.' From that time the condition of the country began to improve, and the happy result was due to the patience as well as the determination of the Governor-General:—

'The difficulties which I encountered in obtaining a correct and consistent account of Tanjore,' he wrote to Dundas, March 5, 1800, 'are scarcely to be described or imagined. After a most tedious inquiry I brought the several contending parties to a fair discussion (or rather to a bitter contest) in my presence; and after an argument which lasted three or four days I proceeded to review the whole case in a regular manner, adverting to every fact and argument on both sides of the question. At length the contending parties unanimously concurred in the expediency and justice of the treaty, in the form in which it has been concluded[1].'

In Surat occurred somewhat similar difficulties and a similar settlement. At that port was the greatest centre of maritime commerce in India, with all the signs of vast trading operations—great wealth, large population, and exceptional jurisdictions. There were strained relations between the Nawáb and the British community. The opportunity of the death of the Nawáb and his son was taken to execute an agreement with the next heir, by which on his succession 'the management and collection of the revenues of the city of Surat and of the territories, places, and other dependencies thereof, the administration of civil and criminal justice, and generally the whole civil and military government of the said

[1] *Wellesley Despatches*, vol. ii. p. 247.

city and its dependencies' were 'vested for ever entirely and exclusively in the honourable English Company[1].'

In these three cases, the Karnátik, Tanjore, and Surat, the essential difficulty with which Wellesley had to cope was the same. This was perceived at home as clearly as in India. Dundas wrote on March 21, 1799, 'The double government existing in the Karnátik has long been felt as a serious calamity to that country'; and it was the same defect of dual control which aggravated the evils of Oriental administration in Tanjore and Surat. It was the age of Union, and Wellesley himself, like his friends at home, was—to employ a modern phrase—an ardent Unionist. In 1799 he had written to Lord Auckland concerning Ireland, 'I trust you will now force a Union.' His feeling in India was the same. It was no love of acquisition or aggression, but the keen desire of the wise administrator for responsible and undivided government.

In Oudh the problem was more complex and the solution more open to criticism. 'Of all Lord Wellesley's dealings,' says a high authority[2], 'his dealings with the Nawáb Wazír of Oudh are apt, at first sight, to seem most harsh and arbitrary.' When fears of an invasion from Zemán Sháh were at their height, Wellesley in 1798 stationed an army in Oudh under the command of Sir James Craig. The Nawáb Wazír,

---

[1] Articles of Agreement, &c., May, 1800; *Wellesley Despatches*, ii. App B.

[2] Mr. Sidney Owen, *Selections from Wellesley Despatches*, p. xvii.

'though fully convinced of the necessity of collecting the largest force upon the frontier, called for a detachment of British troops to attend and guard his person against his own turbulent and disaffected troops. He declared repeatedly that these troops were not to be trusted in the day of battle, or on any service; and after viewing their state of discipline and equipment, and obtaining a knowledge of their principles and attachment to the cause of the allied governments, Sir J. Craig regarded these troops as worse than useless, as dangerous, and of the nature of an enemy's fortress in his rear; and he actually left a detachment of British troops to watch them and the turbulent inhabitants of Rohilkhand, the frontier province of Oudh to the north-west[1].'

The condition of this 'useless rabble,' recognised as it was by Dundas at home as well as by the authorities in India, was not the only reason for interference. The strategical importance of the Doáb, especially at a time when invasion was feared from the Maráthás and Sikhs, as well as from the Afgháns, could hardly be exaggerated. Oudh was the most vulnerable point through which the British settlements could be attacked, and—to take one factor in the situation only—Zemán Sháh was believed to be a real danger, as he certainly was a constant source of alarm. His negotiations with Tipú were known, his movements were unmistakably threatening. A number of his emis-

---

[1] Mr. Sidney Owen, *Selections from Wellesley Despatches* (Sir A. Wellesley's Memorandum), p. lxxxiii.

E

saries had for two or three years visited the provinces of Oudh and Benares, spreading reports of his power[1]; and he had written to Sir John Shore and to Wellesley, declaring his intention of invading Hindustán. The authorities at home had no doubt of the danger. Dundas, writing to Wellesley on March 18, 1799, advised that disturbances should be fomented in his own dominions, that every encouragement should be given to the Sikhs and Rájputs to harass and distress him, and that if possible Sindhia should be definitely engaged in a defensive alliance against him. In face then of this threatened invasion, the position of the Nawáb Wazír was a grave danger. Not only were his frontiers exposed and his troops unmanageable, but his civil administration was hopelessly corrupt. Here, too, Wellesley was not without advice from home. Dundas saw clearly that the needs of Oudh were that the Nawáb Wazír should both organize a just and pure administration of his territory and maintain a permanent and efficient military force. 'This,' he wrote, 'can never be accomplished but by dispersing his useless rabble and forming an army to be kept up and disciplined under our immediate superintendence.'

In a private letter to Mr. Lumsden, December 23, 1798[2], Wellesley sketched his proposals. He desired

---

[1] *Wellesley Despatches*, ii. 55.

[2] *Wellesley Despatches*, i. 386. It is interesting to observe that Wellesley was sketching his future policy towards Oudh at the very time when he might have been thought to have been wholly absorbed by the war with Tipú. This letter was written two days before his departure for Madras.

to acquire the Doáb as a protection alike against Zemán Sháh and the Maráthás, to disband the 'armed rabble which now alarms the Wazír and invites his enemies,' and to substitute an increased force of the Company's infantry and cavalry.

A more delicate matter was the question of the Nawáb's administration. Here it was clear that the wretched man was not himself wholly to blame. The case was not unlike that of the Karnátik. The delight of borrowing money from obliging Europeans had been recklessly indulged in, the country was flooded with needy and unscrupulous adventurers, and the administration was corrupted by the vices alike of East and West. Europeans were eagerly sought for as military officers, swarmed into the country as traders, and throve as money-lenders. Honest commerce had slender sustenance where these leeches had fixed their hold. Wellesley had no mercy for such rascals.

'With respect to the Wazír's civil establishments, and to his abusive systems for the extortion of revenue, and for the violation of every principle of justice, little can be done before I can be enabled to visit Lucknow. I am now under the necessity of proceeding to Fort St. George, whence I trust I shall be at liberty to return to Fort William in the month of March; and I propose to set out for Lucknow at the conclusion of the month of June. I must call your attention to another important subject. The number of Europeans, particularly of British subjects, established in Oudh is a mischief which requires no comment. My resolution is fixed to dislodge every European, excepting the Company's servants, from Oudh. It is my intention to allow to those Europeans now established in Oudh a reasonable time for the settlement of their affairs, limiting the period to twelve or eighteen months at furthest ; you will transmit to me privately a list of all the Europeans now in Oudh, as complete as you can make it, with a statement of their several occupations, and of the period which might reasonably be required by each for settling their affairs. My wish is to occasion as little private distress as possible, but the public service must take its course; and it is not to be expected that some cases of hardship will not be found in the extent of so great a measure.'

It was a bold step, and would create at once a crowd of enemies, ready to take every opportunity of revenge. But on all points of commercial honesty and administrative purity Wellesley was unflinching.

The matters requiring attention were not yet exhausted. The Company's custom of requiring the payment of a British force in the protected country had run here as elsewhere its usual course. By his treaty with Sir John Shore, the Nawáb Saádat Alí was bound to provide seventy-six lacs of rupees per annum to pay 13,000 British troops. This force, it was clear, was too small to be an adequate protection for the extensive territory of Oudh. On November 5, 1799, the Governor-General wrote to the Wazír pointing out this fact, and declaring his opinion that it was impossible for the Company to fulfil its engagement to defend his dominions against all enemies unless it permanently maintained within them an adequate force. By disbanding his rabble the Wazír would be able to pay for the additional British troops, and the change would add greatly to his security. This was no doubt perfectly true; but it clearly placed Oudh more completely under the Company's rule. The Nawáb struggled like a bird in the net. He had several interviews with Colonel Scott, the Resident at Lucknow. At last he suddenly declared his intention to retire from the *masnad*. He was weary, he said, of these recurring difficulties; he had no responsible advisers, he would be rid of the whole business.

It was evidently an astonishing proposition to the staid British colonel; but the Nawáb was insistent, and the Resident applied to Wellesley for instructions. The Governor-General wrote at once to the Directors, and directed Colonel William Kirkpatrick[1] to reply to the Resident. Is it unnatural to infer that he regarded the prospect with elation? It was another addition to those events which would make his rule an epoch in the history of British India. But if he felt pride he studiously concealed it. He declared, as to the abdication, that he neither wished nor approved it, but if it must be it should be on conditions which alone could make it satisfactory to the British government. In a long minute[2] (December 16, 1799) he dwelt impressively on the overwhelming difficulties

---

[1] His military secretary; another of the able family already noticed.
[2] *Wellesley Despatches*, ii. 159-167.

under which the Nawáb's successor would labour. His burdens would be greater, his fitness to meet them indubitably less. Every aspect of the situation pointed to the solution which Wellesley believed, in every similar case, to be the best. Where the responsibility was, there must be the control. A dual government was hopeless : the new Nawáb then must reign, but not govern. Did not the Nawáb himself recognise the necessity of this course ?

'The same wisdom and penetration which have opened to his Excellency's view the real nature of the embarrassments in which he is involved, and convinced him of his inability to extricate himself by his own exertions, will equally satisfy him that evils of such magnitude and inveteracy cannot be remedied otherwise than by the gradual and regular operation of a system of administration founded on principles of substantial justice and of true policy, and enforced by all the power and energy of the British Government. It must be obvious to his Excellency that the immediate accession of his eldest or of any of his sons to the *masnad* would be altogether incompatible with the establishment of such a system. What rational hope could be entertained that any of these young princes would be competent to the correction of those evils which his Excellency himself, aided by all his knowledge and experience of public affairs, has confessed himself unable to remedy. Under the administration of a successor destitute of his Excellency's experience and knowledge, all the existing evils in the state and condition of the country of Oudh would, of necessity, be augmented, and with the rapid increase of every abuse in the civil and military government, the danger of the country from foreign enemies, and the domestic misery of the inhabitants would be aggravated in an equal proportion. Long and severe experience has manifested the inefficacy of any partial or indirect interference of the British Government for the reform of the administration of Oudh. The same causes which have hitherto frustrated every endeavour of the Company's Government to accomplish that salutary object by the mere effect of advice and admonition, would continue to operate under every divided Government. No beneficial result can be expected from the utmost endeavours of the wisdom and justice of the Company, whilst another power shall exist in the country to exclude the introduction of every salutary reform or to counteract its operation.'

The government of Oudh, he went on, could never be administered with advantage without the direct introduction of British power; nor would any temporary arrangement be effectual: divided administration is fatal. And since the Wazír seems convinced that only British authority can restore public order, internal tranquillity or external strength, 'the Governor-General advises the Nawáb Wazír to vest the exclusive administration of the civil and military government of Oudh and its dependencies in the hands of the Company, with such ample powers as shall enable the Company to act with vigour and promptitude in every branch and department of State.'

This was by no means to the Wazír's mind. Ease and retirement he affected to desire—probably only with the intention of protracting negotiations and seeing at the least what he might gain by the transaction. But the surrender of all power to the Company—that was another matter. Before long

Wellesley wrote to the Directors [1]: 'I have now every reason to believe that the proposition of the Nawáb Wazír to abdicate the sovereignty of his dominions was illusory from the commencement, and designed to defeat, by artificial delays, the proposed reform of his Excellency's military establishments.'

The Wazír had chosen the wrong man to trifle with. Wellesley had certainly not originated—he had not even encouraged—the suggested abdication; but when it was made it must be adhered to, or at least an arrangement must be made which would confer corresponding benefits on the Company. On February 9, he wrote to 'communicate' in the most unqualified terms, the astonishment, regret, and indignation which 'the Wazír's recent conduct had excited' in his mind. The letter was one of those cold, impressive indictments which Wellesley knew so well how to draw. The whole course of the proceedings is sketched in bold and forcible lines; and then the indignant Governor-General does not hesitate to charge 'a person of your Excellency's high rank and exalted dignity,' directly and in so many words with the offence of which he had already declared him guilty in his letter to the Secret Committee.

There must be no playing with the British Government. There must be no delay: two urgent and indispensable works must be undertaken at once—the reform of the army and the proper support of the

[1] Jan. 25, 1800. *Wellesley Despatches*, ii. 195.

Company's troops in Oudh.—If not, be the peril yours.—'The least omission or procrastination in either of those important points must lead to the most serious mischief.'

The plans that had been matured when the abdication was believed to be real were not stopped when it proved to be a sham. Troops had been ordered to Oudh: not a day was their march delayed; and the Nawáb was warned that he must pay and feed them. Then there was what Carlyle was fond of calling a 'pause of an awful nature:' but the Wazír hurried not with the abdication or his subsidy. It was ill dallying with Wellesley: his terms grew harder, like the Sibyl's, by waiting. On January 22, 1801, he wrote to Colonel Scott that he offered to the Nawáb a treaty exactly similar to that made with the Rájá of Tanjore. If he should reject it, he must clearly understand that he still must pay for the augmented force of British troops, and to secure the payment must surrender to the Company in perpetual sovereignty an adequate portion of his territory. The Doáb must be surrendered, and Rohilkhand, so as to surround the remains of the principality by a ring-fence of the Company's possessions. Between these let the hesitating Wazír make his choice: but he must choose promptly.

This to Colonel Scott, and with equal vigour and directness to the Wazír himself. Another letter came from the Wazír, trying his utmost to shake himself free. Then, on April 5, a stern reply from

Wellesley, again quoting the repeated statements of the Wazír himself, again describing the wretched condition of the country and the benefits to be expected from British rule. 'You will show your regard for the interests of your family and your people by despatching a prompt reply accepting one or other of the alternatives.' To Colonel Scott a further despatch met the contention of the Nawáb, that so long as his payments were made punctually no territorial cession was needed, by the answer that 'it is evident that to refrain from demanding adequate security until the resources of the country shall actually have failed, would be to defeat all expectation of attaining the security to which the Company is entitled. . . . His Excellency,' he adds, 'has virtually destroyed the force of any argument founded on the punctuality of his payments by admitting the ruinous state of the country, by acknowledging his apprehension of an impending failure of his resources and by declaring his own incompetency to remove the causes of those evils.' If the Nawáb should still reject both propositions, his time of repentance was past, and Scott was to require the immediate cession of the districts or to send British troops at once to take possession of them. Once again the Nawáb struggled convulsively: he sent articles to the Governor-General. They were sternly rejected, and the Resident was instructed to proceed to compulsion.

Thus the whole gamut of diplomacy had been run through, and from the retort courteous the opponents had risen to the countercheck quarrelsome. Another method was now adopted. On July 5, 1801, the Governor-General instructed the Hon. Henry Wellesley to proceed at once to Lucknow, with full power to conclude a treaty in concert with Colonel Scott on the lines of the previous offers, and with instructions to conclude the matter with rapidity. Before he arrived the Nawáb turned from passive to active and obstinate refusal; he declined to pay any further subsidies.

Henry Wellesley reached Lucknow in September, and the Nawáb after some parley consented to treat. The Governor-General determined to clinch matters by visiting Oudh himself: but while his state-barge was at the mouth of the Gumtí he heard that the Nawáb had yielded and the treaty had been signed.

He wrote at once to the Directors[1]:—

'The Nawáb has ceded in perpetuity and in full sovereignty to the honourable Company the territories enumerated in the statements which I have the honour to enclose.'

'It is my intention,' he added, 'immediately to appoint a temporary administration for the settlement of the ceded districts. This provisional government will be composed of several of the most experienced, able, and active of the Company's civil servants in the departments of judicature, commerce, and revenue, and will be presided over by Mr. Henry Wellesley, to whose discretion, address, and firmness the Company is principally indebted for the early and tranquil settlement of these extensive and fertile territories.'

[1] *Wellesley Despatches*, vol. ii. p. 597.

Thus the objects which Wellesley had in view seemed to be securely attained. The territories ceded formed a barrier between the dominions of the Wazír and any foreign enemy; and he undertook to carry out such an administration in his own dominions as should conduce to the happiness and prosperity of his people. Oudh seemed safe, and ought to be well governed. The Governor-General wrote, a month later, to the Directors, putting concisely the benefits which he expected to accrue from the settlement of Oudh. He had during his progress been everywhere struck with the flourishing and happy condition of the provinces under British rule. It was thus with no common satisfaction that he was able to substitute for the iniquitous system of the Nawáb, which had been sustained solely by the power of the British sword, 'the salutary influence of those regulations and laws of which' he had recently 'witnessed and admired the practical wisdom and extensive benevolence.'

He went on to Lucknow, and there, having gained his ends, treated the Nawáb with all courtesy and respect. Daily conferences, with a dignified hospitality, seemed to smooth the remaining difficulties; and Wellesley could write that he looked forward to a tranquil settlement of the North-West Provinces during the year 1802, and, in the March of that year, that it had already proceeded beyond his most sanguine expectations. Thus the Wazír and his rabble-rout might vanish for ever from the anxious dreams of the British ruler.

Wellesley evidently expected that his conduct would be cordially approved at home. He had increased at once the extent and the security of the Company's possessions; and he had added to their revenue, a point which generally condoned in their eyes for any breach of their orders. But the Directors were already alienated from their Governor-General by his action in the matter of private trade and by his demand of a superior education for their civil servants; and they were not disposed to look upon his policy in Oudh with favourable eyes. Among the MSS. of the India Office lies a paper of charges against the Governor-General in this relation[1], which unquestionably represents a very considerable body of English opinion. After a lengthy record of facts it ends thus :—

'The inferences which may be drawn from the preceding narrative and observations appear to be—1st, that the introduction of an additional number of troops into the Wazír's territories was an infraction of existing treaties, inasmuch that such augmentation was not only not required or demanded by the Wazír, but that his acquiescence therein was extorted; 2nd, that the demand of territorial security for the payment of the subsidy and the arrears on account of the augmented force was not warranted by the treaty of 1778, as the kists of the subsidy were not in arrear, nor did ever the treaty require the Wazír to give security for arrears of the description demanded; 3rd, that the territory ceded by the Treaty of Lucknow in 1801 was violently and compulsorily wrested from the Wazír, as he not only decidedly and

[1] India Office Record Department MSS., Fisher Papers, 256 (1776).

unequivocally rejected the proposition for a territorial cession, as well as that for an absolute abandonment of the sovereignty of his country, but that the Governor-General, having repeatedly declared his firm determination never to recede from his demand of territorial cession, and even twice threatened the assumption of certain districts, he at length gave a reluctant assent, declaring that he never could of himself consent to either proposition, but that he had no alternative but passive obedience to whatever measure the Governor-General might resolve on, and finally, he considered it as a disgrace and that it would be highly unpleasant to him to show his face to his subjects; 4th, that as the Treaty of Lucknow concluded by Mr. Wellesley in 1801 was never cordially accepted by the Wazír but on the contrary it was a measure absolutely forced upon him, the stipulation in the 6th article, whereby the Wazír is bound to abide by the advice and counsel of the Company's officers in the administration of the affairs of his internal government of his reserved dominion, is a breach of Lord Cornwallis's treaty of 1787 and of the Treaty of Lucknow, 1798, in both of which it is stipulated that the Company will not interfere with the internal regulation of the Nawáb's government, but that he shall be left in full possession of his authority over his household affairs, hereditary dominions, his troops and subjects.'

Charges such as these would probably not have been sufficient to lose for their servant the favour of the Court. High dividends and reasonable security —these were both increased rather than diminished by Wellesley's high-handed action. But he had forgotten that if the proprietors were solicitous about their interest they were still more insistent upon their patronage. It was the patronage question which had wrecked the India Bill of Mr. Fox and overthrown his ministry. It was Pitt's attitude towards their patronage which had gained him much of his support. And now the Governor-General, their servant, had appointed to a most important and lucrative office his own brother, who was not in their employment— 'a virtual supersession of the just rights of' their own civilians. They would hear no reason, they would wait for no report: they directed 'that Mr. Wellesley be removed forthwith.' Happily the Board of Control knew better than thus to dictate. in a matter comparatively so trifling, to a man in whose hands rested so vast a responsibility; they at least would not treat the Governor-General as if he were a corrupt postmaster or exciseman; and they prohibited for the present any decision of the Company on the appointment.

The correspondence between the Board of Control and the Directors was sent to the Governor-General. If anything could have further alienated him from the present rulers of Leadenhall Street, it cannot be doubted that it would be their crowning act of personal distrust. They had again and again thwarted him, it will be seen, in his public policy; here was an unpardonable slight upon his private honour. The subsequent career of Henry Wellesley, afterwards Lord Cowley, was more than a sufficient justification of his brother's favour. His conduct of the negotiations with the Wazír had been marked by a singular union of firmness and tact. And—if it be necessary to make even the slightest allusion to the basest suggestion—he had refused all emolument beyond that due to him as private secretary to the Governor-General. As soon as the settlement of Oudh was accomplished he resigned the post for which he had been so well qualified.

It has been questioned whether our rule over the ceded districts was beneficial, and it has been denied that the English intervention much improved in the long run the condition of the country. This was not Sir Arthur Wellesley's opinion. He stated, in his memorandum referred to above, that the Nawáb had already (in 1806) felt the full benefit of the Company's obligation to defend him, in the ease with which he collected a larger revenue than before, and the more satisfactory condition of his troops and his administration. Questions such as these would, however, need for their satisfactory solution an extended discussion: but one thing at least is clear—the difficulties which occurred in putting down the local tyrants and petty chieftains, before any system of regular taxation, jurisdiction, or administration could be set up, are proofs, patent enough, of the state of anarchy from which it is unquestionable that British rule delivered the ceded districts. Of Oudh itself it is less easy to speak: but Wellesley himself, if he could have lived in the time of the Mutiny, would probably have asserted that its condition in our own day proved that his error had been, not that he took part, but that he did not take the whole.

But, after all, the one cardinal justification of Wellesley's policy towards Oudh lies, not in any benefit to the population or in an extension of the Company's territory or revenue, but in an absolute political necessity. Those who would estimate his action justly must be content to rest their conclusion entirely on that ground. The high-handed conduct of the negotiations, the lengthy and not wholly illuminative character of the Governor-General's minutes and letters, may be the legitimate objects of severe criticism; but it is not with them that the true issue lies. Wellesley found Oudh a pressing and unmistakable danger to the British position in India: he left it a safeguard and a support.

CHAPTER V

WELLESLEY AND THE MARÁTHÁS[1]

IF the Mysore conquest was the most glorious and memorable feature of Wellesley's administration it was the Maráthá war which taxed his powers to the utmost and tested his claims to be considered a statesman of the first order. The condition of the Maráthá confederacy, a volcano bursting now and again into active and dangerous eruption, was the most complex problem that he was called upon to meet. The solution which he offered was not accepted at the time. The execution of his policy was attended by disasters for which he was not responsible but of which he had to bear the blame. It was condemned, repudiated, reversed. But in the long run his principles had again to be brought forward, and what might have been carried out under happier auspices in 1805 was at last accomplished by another hand in 1818.

In his first despatches home Wellesley had shown that he had grasped the complexity of the Maráthá problem. Was it desirable that there should be a sort of balance between the different branches of that

---

[1] Among other authorities Wellesley's *Notes Relative to the late Transactions in the Marhatta Empire*, Fort William, Dec., 1803, should be observed.

loose confederacy? Was its weakness to be approved or arrested? He considered it incontestable that the Peshwá's power had declined greatly—never was his influence so inconsiderable: that Sindhia also had lost much of the power which the great Mahadájí had held; that the territory of Holkar, torn by dynastic strife, had passed out of count in the political system; that Bhonsla only—and he was traditionally our friend—had risen in the scale.

The estimate was not altogether accurate. Daulat Ráo Sindhia, threatened by the insurrection of the Bais (three widows of his predecessor), had called in the aid of his prisoner, the aged and astute Nána Farnavis. Nána resumed the position of chief minister at Poona, and there was an appearance of cordiality between the Peshwá and Sindhia. But the futile and vacillating policy which seemed natural to the Marátha counsels lost the opportunity which the Mysore war might have given. Up to the last the Peshwá publicly received the envoys of Tipú; his troops took no part in the campaign, and the treaty, and with it the territory offered by the victors, was rejected. Sindhia was still harassed by the insurrections; Bhonsla was approached by Wellesley with a view to a treaty on the lines of that with the Nizám: and the beginning of the nineteenth century found the English face to face with the Maráthás, and, as it seemed, with the Peshwá for the time the only power with whom it would be profitable seriously to bargain.

The general policy on which Wellesley had acted was clearly applicable to this as to the other cases with which he had had to deal. British supremacy must be asserted over all the States with which the Company was brought in contact: and in all disputes between provinces the British government must be arbiter. Negotiations proceeded slowly. Nána struggled to keep such power as remained to the Peshwá free at least from European control: he was strenuously opposed to the admission of any English troops. 'He respected the English,' says Grant Duff, 'he admired their sincerity and the vigour of their government, but as political enemies no one regarded them with more jealousy and alarm.' In his old age he still clung to the phantom of Marátha independence, and, to his honour, he strove to moderate the passions which would turn against each other the weapons which the Marátha chieftains should have used only on their foes. But he died, at a great age as it seemed for an Indian statesman in days when the dagger and poison were common resorts for the settlement of political difficulties, on March 13, 1800. 'With him,' wrote Colonel Palmer the British Resident at Poona, 'has departed all the wisdom and moderation of the Marátha government.'

Then began a scramble for power in which it was not only prudent but necessary for the English to intervene. The opportunity was given through the part played by Jeswant Ráo Holkar in the events of the time. On the death, in 1795, of Túkají Ráo

Holkar, who had ruled in Indore with Ahalya Bái, his sons, legitimate and illegitimate, fought with each other and with Sindhia for the remnants of his power. Murder, rapine, and the most fiendish methods of execution, such as trampling to death by infuriated elephants, were freely employed. Finally Jeswant Ráo, the ablest and not the most scrupulous of the sons, emerged from the butchery and confusion with a force of adventurers and freebooters, Indian and Afghán, ravaging the territories of Sindhia.

Fortune changed sides again and again : now Holkar was uppermost, now Sindhia : and the wretched Peshwá, Bájí Ráo, was the mere sport of the contending factions. Campaign and intrigue rose and fell in bewildering alternation; and the British residents, first Palmer and then Close, mingled with the warring chieftains, offering terms and treaties. It was ill treating with parties who knew not what the day might bring forth : but at length a decisive event threw the ball into Wellesley's hands. On October 25, 1802, Holkar defeated, with every completeness, the forces of the Peshwá and of Sindhia before Poona. He entered the city, placed Warnak Ráo, a tame claimant for the office of Peshwá, upon the *masnad*, and acted for two months with moderation in the hope of some diplomatic guarantee of his position. Colonel Close was fortunate enough to be able to leave Poona in safety on September 28. Meanwhile Bájí Ráo had fled, and after some hesitation, placed himself in the hands of the

English. On December 6 he reached Bassein. and before the end of the month the treaty of Bassein was signed. By its provisions six battalions of infantry, with the usual proportion of field artillery and European artillerymen, were to be permanently stationed in the Peshwá's dominions—a force which was to be increased in time of war—two thousand men being attached to the Peshwá's person. For the payment of these troops, districts yielding twenty-six lacs of rupees were ceded to the Company in perpetuity. The Peshwá agreed to enter upon no treaties and make no war upon other states without previous consultation with the British Government; and, as an earnest of this arrangement, he referred all his claims upon the Gáekwár and the Nizám to English arbitration.

The far-reaching results of this famous treaty could not be concealed. At once the Marátha forces showed signs of closing together to resist the foreigner. Sindhia and Bhonsla began to treat, Holkar to strengthen his defences. It was without question a step which changed entirely the footing on which we stood in Western India. It trebled the English responsibilities in an instant. It made English interests no longer subordinate but supreme in this quarter of the vast Peninsula, as they had already become in the South, North, and East. 'Previously to the treaty,' says Mr. Sidney Owen—and no living authority is more competent to speak—'there existed a British Empire *in* India: the treaty, by its direct or indirect operations, gave the Company the Empire *of* India¹.'

From the first the arrangement was exposed to severe, even violent, criticism. ' Lord Castlereagh, whose knowledge of the affairs of India was not so great as his vigour in expressing it, wrote sharp strictures on the treaty. He denied the necessity of mingling in the Marátha conflicts. Till Tipú fell, he said, we needed, or might need, Marátha aid; but now it could be no more than a safeguard against remote and contingent dangers. And as for their own interest, it made wholly against the alliance. 'To talk to them of the advantages of our guarantee for preserving the peace of Hindustán, assumes that the genius of their government is industrious and pacific instead of being predatory and hostile.' A broader connection might have been formed if Sindhia and Holkar had been suffered to destroy each other before we made treaty with the Peshwá. Now it is more than probable that it will lead to immediate war, certain that it will immerse us in constant and vexatious intrigue. ' Much of my doubt,' says Castlereagh, upon the policy of any Marátha treaty, however modified, arises from an apprehension of its tendency to involve us too much in the endless and complicated distractions of that turbulent empire.' And for the same reason he thought that the right of arbitration between the Peshwá and other States should be abandoned.

[1] *Selections from the Wellington Despatches*, Introduction, p. xlvi.

Such, briefly, was the purport of Castlereagh's strictures. Non-intervention, again and again, is the policy echoed at Whitehall; and the only reply that could be made was that it was impossible. The Directors harped upon the same string. The subsidiary force must on no account be allowed to enter the Peshwá's dominions except on his special requisition. It must remain within the Company's territories—a proposal which would probably be less satisfactory to the Peshwá than that of the treaty itself, since he was still expected to pay for its support. But the timidity of the Directors peeps out still more in the suggestions as to the war, which had now begun—'Although we have thought it right to advert to the possible expediency of requiring certain sacrifices in the nature of reparation from our opponents, you are by no means to consider such suggestions as controlling your conduct in case you should be of opinion under all the circumstances that peace is likely to be more firmly established by an entire restoration of all our conquests.' There is something grotesquely humorous in the suggestion that Wellesley would see fit to restore all conquests: one can hardly help suspecting the dull old traders of a cumbrous jocularity.

The 'philosophical historian' is still more severe in his judgement. Mill's criticisms resolve themselves into two propositions—first, that the treaty of necessity produced war; and second, that it was not worth the cost. 'The good things derived from the treaty of Bassein must be regarded as all summed up in these two effects—first, the war with the Marátha chiefs; and secondly, the means which it contributed to the success of the war.' These means Mill counts, not unfairly, as slight. But his main contention is incorrect. The treaty of Bassein did not create the war. War would probably have occurred in any case sooner or later. The treaty of Bassein enabled it to be carried on with better chances of success.

The strictures of Castlereagh were answered by Arthur Wellesley, now Major-General. Castlereagh, he points out with his usual directness, did not understand the political condition of India. French influence was still to be feared and to be guarded against. 'In the consideration of every question of Indian policy or in an enquiry into the expediency of any political measure, it is absolutely necessary to view it not only as it will affect Indian powers, but as it will affect the French.' French influence may appear to us now to have been scarcely serious; but Wellesley was right; so long as General Perron commanded a French force at the camp of Sindhia it would have been criminal to ignore the possibilities of French intervention [1]. The future conqueror of Napoleon had

[1] 'The views of France would have been materially favoured by the strength and efficiency of Monsieur Perron's force, established with great territorial dominion, extending towards the left bank of the Indus, through the Punjáb, and comprehending Agra, Delhi, and a large portion of the Doáb, of the Jumna, and Ganges, on the most vulnerable part of our north-western frontier of Hindustán, and holding the person and nominal authority of the unfortunate Sháh 'Alám (the deposed Mughal Emperor) in the most abject and degrading subjection.' *Wellesley Despatches*, iii. xxx.

already fixed his gaze on the contest which was to be the most glorious feature of his life.

As to the actual consequences upon our relations with the Maráthás, war with Holkar, he argued, but for the treaty of Bassein would have been nearly certain and probably would have included all the Marátha states. But the strongest political defence of the treaty—opposed to the arguments of Castlereagh and the Directors alike—lies in the obligation which it lays upon the Peshwá to treat and make war only on the Company's advice. 'This article is the bond of peace to India. It is this which renders the treaty really a defensive one and makes the Governor-General genuinely responsible for every war in which the British Government may be engaged. If this article were not in the treaty, the Peshwá would be the responsible person.' Such was the defence of the hard-headed soldier who, it must be noted, did not approve of the general principles upon which his brother acted in this and other treaties.

The treaty did not lack defence from Indian administrators of eminence. Among these was Mr. Barlow, afterwards himself for a while Governor-General, and by no means a blind supporter of Wellesley's policy. He wrote a note to the Governor-General strongly supporting the treaty. The question, he states clearly, lay in a nutshell. When the Peshwá had sought our assistance, should we repudiate our old connection with him and refuse him aid? To refuse would have been alike impolitic and base. To give involved the action which ensued. And, on the wider issue—'It is absolutely necessary for the defeat of [the French] designs that no native state should be left to exist in India which is not upheld by the British power, or the political conduct of which is not under its absolute control.' Here is asserted more strongly than Wellesley had as yet asserted it, the claim—and the necessity—of Britain to be supreme in India. It was the empire *of* India, Barlow truly saw, which must be ours.

So far objections to the treaty of Bassein may be considered and answered. But there remains the further question, which is involved in the whole network of Wellesley's rule, of subsidiary alliance in general. If it be wise to support and subsidize native princes, we are bound so to treat with the Peshwá. But is it wise to support and subsidize at all?

Arthur Wellesley, though he had approved the treaty in the main, and that for important reasons, had doubts after a while as to its efficacy, and these doubts were based on distrust of the system. 'One bad consequence of these subsidiary treaties,' he writes to Malcolm in June, 1803, 'is that they entirely annihilate the military power of the governments with which we contract them ... and their reliance for defence is exclusively on us... I would preserve the existence of the State, and guide its actions by the weight of British influence rather than annihilate it and establish new powers in India by the subsidiary treaty[1].' Writing

[1] To Major Malcolm. Owen's *Selections from Wellington Despatches*, 244.

a year later, he noted that such treaties reduced the strength of the powers with which we were connected, but he pointed out the enormous benefits that they conferred. 'The consequences of them have been that in this war with the Maráthás, which it is obvious must have occurred sooner or later, the Company's territories have not been invaded; and the evils of war have been kept at a distance from the sources of our wealth and our power. This fact alone, unsupported by any others which could be enumerated as benefits resulting from these alliances, would be sufficient to justify them [1].'

It may be concluded then, that General Wellesley summed up on the whole in favour of the treaty; and from his conversation in later years this may be taken to be the case. For the Peshwá Grant Duff remarks that it was the only course open—his only refuge from becoming the absolute puppet of one or other of the chiefs. Himself the deputy of a shadowy and impotent prince, the Rájá of Sátára, he might have sunk to be the mere phantom of a phantom. The result of the treaty to his people was seen, said Malcolm, a keen observer, in the dawn of tranquillity, prosperity, and peace.

It was, however, peace only through war. Sindhia and Bhonsla began almost at once to ally. Sindhia saw in the treaty of Bassein and the submission of the Peshwá to English influence the sure beginning of the last fight of the Maráthás for existence. As

---

[1] To Major Shawe. Owen's *Selections from Wellington Despatches*, p. 464.

surely as in the old days their claim to *chauth* had destroyed the Mughal power, so surely would they be destroyed in their turn by the acceptance of subsidiary alliances. He turned to Holkar and endeavoured to induce him to combine against the English: but some sluggishness or blindness weighed that chieftain down, and he retired to Málwá and waited in anxious inaction for the issue of events. On May 13, 1803, under General Wellesley's protection, Bájí Ráo re-entered Poona. Wellesley was appointed political agent as well as military commander, and at once brought matters to a crisis. Would Sindhia and Bhonsla retire to their territories in peace? They would not. Then war must be the result. On August 3, Colonel Collins, the British agent, left Sindhia's camp, and this was taken as the declaration of war.

From this moment events moved rapidly. Everything had been planned with the forethought and wisdom which were the marks of Wellesley's greatness. The objects of the Governor-General were, as in the Mysore war, clearly defined. He desired 'to conquer the whole of that portion of Sindhia's dominions which lay between the Ganges and the Jumna, destroying completely the French force by which the frontier was protected, extending the Company's frontier to the Jumna, and including the cities of Delhi and Agra, with a chain of forts sufficient for protecting the navigation of the river, on the right bank of the river.' This was only part of a plan which included the assumption by the Company of a defensible if not a scientific frontier. Bundelkhand was to be acquired, or at least so much of it as would secure the hold on Agra, and in Gujarát, Baroch with the district round it, long coveted by the Council of Bombay, and in the East the province of Cuttack, to connect Madras with Bengal. Wellesley further intended to secure the person of the aged Sháh'Alám the 'Emperor,' who had long been under the control of Sindhia.

To effect these objects, nearly 50,000 men were assembled. In Gujarát the results of Colonel Murray's movements and Major Walker's diplomacy will be mentioned in another connection. The capture of Cuttack by Colonel Harcourt may be dismissed with equal brevity. Both point to the accuracy of Wellesley's estimate of the means required to carry out his ends. Bundelkhand was taken with equal ease. The serious conflicts were in the Deccan and in Hindustán.

General Wellesley, with about 9,000 men, and Colonel Stevenson, with nearly 8,000, were left to undertake operations in the Deccan. On August 8, Wellesley advanced to Ahmadnagar, and captured it in four days. From thence he advanced to Aurangábád, and then down the left bank of the Godávari till he came to the Kaitna, which he crossed, and met the whole combined army of Sindhia and Bhonsla on September 23, at Assaye. The story of the fight has been told so often, and so well, that there is no need to dwell upon it. In the words of the General himself—simplest and most direct—

'We attacked immediately and the troops advanced under a very hot fire ... The enemy's cavalry made an attempt to charge the 74th Regiment at the moment when they were most exposed to this fire, but they were cut up by the British cavalry which moved on at that moment. At length the enemy's line gave way in all directions, and the British cavalry cut in among their broken infantry; but some of their corps went off in good order, and a fire was kept up on our troops from many of the guns, from which the enemy had been first driven, by individuals who had been passed by the line under the supposition that they were dead.

'Lieut.-Colonel Maxwell, with the British cavalry, charged one large body of infantry, which had retired and was formed again, in which operation he was killed; and some time elapsed before we could put an end to the straggling fire which was kept up by individuals from the guns from which the enemy were driven. The enemy's cavalry also, which had been hovering round us throughout the action, was still near us. At length, when the last formed body of infantry gave way, the whole went off and left in our hands ninety pieces of cannon[1].'

This victory, as the first great battle in which the conqueror of Waterloo was victorious, has been celebrated with even more jubilation than is proportionate to the other achievements of the war, but it was undoubtedly a great feat and a glorious victory. The enemy's troops were at least ten times the number of the British, and they had the advantage of French training and of considerable French contingents.

It was, says an enthusiastic soldier, 'a triumph

---

[1] Major-General Wellesley to the Governor-General. *Wellesley Despatches*, vol. iii. p. 325.

more splendid than any recorded in Deccan history [1].'
It was followed up by the victory of Argáon on
November 29, over Bhonsla, a battle even more
decisive than the last. On December 14, General
Wellesley stormed the great fortress of Gáwilgarh.
With this the war in the Deccan ended, and Bhonsla
yielded completely. On December 17, General
Wellesley exchanged the sword for the pen, and
Bhonsla signed the treaty of Deogáon, by which he
accepted all the terms, except that of a resident force,
which the Peshwá had accepted for himself. He was
to receive a British resident at Nágpur, to entertain
no subjects of any country at war with Britain, and
to give up all claims of *chauth* against the Nizám,
submitting all his disputes to English decision. And
in addition he gave up Cuttack, and all the land west
of the Wardhá river, a district given to the Nizám.

The campaign in Hindustán had been equally
brilliant. General Lake had a force of about 10,000
men. Opposed to him was the French-drilled army
led by M. Perron. This large body of men had been
brought together originally by General Count de
Boigne—a brilliant adventurer, without that spice of
the brigand which often attaches to the name—and
had formed the pride and the safeguard of the great
Mahádají Sindhia. The great chief was dead, and his
trusty captain had returned to France, but the troops
were held together, and, with districts secured for their
support, formed a kind of military colony under the

[1] Grant Duff, vol. iii. p. 243.

command of M. Perron. But it was a dangerous and unsatisfactory post to be captain of free companies to a vindictive and treacherous Oriental, and Perron was already sick of it. He had made overtures to the English for facilities to retire, and Wellesley had offered him every assistance. Now it came to war he could not fly; he turned to fight the course, but, it may be, with a faint heart.

It needed only a few weeks' skirmishing and the capture by Lake of the strong town of Alígarh, on September 4, to end the Frenchman's indecision. He applied for leave to pass through the English lines, which Lake readily granted, and so he passed out of history, 'a man of plain sense, of no talent, but a brave soldier,' as de Boigne described him to Grant Duff. His place was taken by a younger officer, M. Louis Bourquin, who crossed the Jumna to meet Lake, with the intention of preventing his advance to Delhi. A fierce battle took place on September 11, outside the city, when brilliant charges of cavalry swept the troops of Sindhia from the field. Delhi was entered in triumph, and the aged 'Emperor' was released from thraldom and placed under new masters who behaved very handsomely to him. M. Bourquin surrendered with a number of his men three days after the battle, and then the French military interest in India practically ceased to be.

From Delhi Lake marched to Agra, and on October 18 it surrendered. A decisive battle took place on the 31st at Laswári, where the main body of Sindhia's remaining troops met Lake. It was a matter of hard fighting and great slaughter. In the end the British charges carried all before them, and the French contingents of Sindhia were captured or annihilated. This battle ended the war. Sindhia had no longer an army: he could no more use the shadowy name of the Mughal to call troops to his banner. Bhonsla had been defeated and had made peace. There was no course open to him but submission.

On December 30, the treaty of Surji Arjangáon was signed. By this Sindhia ceded all the territory between the Jumna and the Ganges, Ahmadnagar (which was given to the Peshwá), his rights over Baroch (as already mentioned), and all the land north of Jaipur, Jadhpur and Gohad. He renounced all claims upon the English and their allies, and agreed to entertain no subject of any nation at war with them, and to recognise the rights of several of the Rájput chiefs whose cause Lake had espoused. Soon after Sindhia submitted to a modified form of the subsidiary alliance.

Thus peace seemed to have been secured, and Wellesley wrote one of the letters that were become so familiar, enumerating and tabulating the results which he thought would spring from the war. The military power of Sindhia and of Bhonsla was now no longer a menace to the East India Company. The French territorial possessions were destroyed, and British influence was established in the North-West and with the *éclat* that the name of Sháh 'Alám was still able to bestow. The territorial acquisitions added at once to British security and British power; and the government was now established in connection with every principal state in India. All this in the bald and business-like style which Wellesley now affected to the Directors. In a reply to an enthusiastic address of the inhabitants of Calcutta an old vein reasserts itself:—

'With united counsels, with an unrivalled army, with flourishing resources, with powerful alliances, and with a just cause, I was enabled to encounter and to surmount the difficulties which surrounded me, and to witness the rapid and complete effect of our military operations on every point of the enemy's strength. The vast extent, complicated system, and matchless success of the campaigns in Hindustán and the Deccan cannot be contemplated without emotions of gratitude and admiration. The execution of the plans, which it was my duty to form, corresponded with the renown of an army, accustomed to victory, inured to fatigue and danger, attached to the first principles of discipline and order, animated by the memory of former triumphs, and commanded by generals who possess every qualification requisite to inspire confidence, to excite enterprise and to ensure success. Peace is the fairest fruit of victory, the brightest ornament of military triumph, and the highest reward of successful valour. The peace which has been concluded comprehends every object of the war with every practicable security for the continuance of tranquillity.'

The Governor-General was too hasty. The fruits of peace were not yet ripe. While he spoke war was brewing, and before May, 1804, Holkar had already taken up arms. Thus the claims which Wellesley made for the results of his action were not justified; and criticisms on the whole policy were beginning to reach him from home.

Castlereagh had already begun to question. He wrote (May 21, 1804) in the tone of deference which it is clear that the extraordinary brilliancy of Wellesley's achievements had begun to inspire. But he insinuated two doubts. Was the policy of annexation permissible on the principles which Parliament had sanctioned? Would not the extent of territory and interest be too great a burden for any ordinary ruler? 'We should deceive ourselves if we expected to find a successor to replace your Lordship capable of giving and continuing to the machine of government that impulse which every department of the state so visibly receives from the mind that now directs it.'

But criticism soon succeeded compliment, and question became condemnation. At the end of the year 1803, General Lake, under Wellesley's instructions, began to negotiate with Holkar, and considerable correspondence ensued between them. On December 28, Lake, writing to the Governor-General, observed the 'extraordinary conduct' of Holkar; his 'levying contribution and otherwise distressing the country,' and his having 'lately put to death the English officers in his service, Captains Vickars, Todd, and Ryan.' Wellesley still thought peace was probable, and believed that Holkar would readily agree to it as soon as he knew of the treaty with Sindhia. But he was entirely deceived. The customs of Marátha policy needed no such explicit declaration of hostility as Europeans looked for, and it is clear from the Memoirs of Muhammad Amír Khán, a Pindári leader, in alliance with Holkar, that from the moment of the Peshwá's submission all the other Marátha chiefs were cordially allied against the British. Circumstances had prevented the appearance of his troops on the field—they were actually on the march at the time of Assaye—but Holkar had not abandoned his compatriots[1].

Thus Wellesley's negotiations were futile, and on April 16 the Governor-General issued orders to Generals Lake and Wellesley to begin the war. Lake was to move from Delhi with the army of Hindustán, and Colonel Murray was to advance from Gujarát against Holkar's possessions in Málwá: Sindhia was instructed to join in the reduction of his rival's territories.

At first all went well. Rámpura, Holkar's stronghold in the north, was taken on May 16, and Holkar retreated in hot haste. General Wellesley urged Lake to pursue him or to withdraw with all his forces to Hindustán during the rains. Unhappily he did neither. He retired to Cawnpore, and he sent Colonel Monson on with five battalions of native infantry, some artillery, and about 4,000 irregular horse to keep Holkar in check, and, as it appears, to advance

[1] See Mill's *India*, vol. vi. p. 399, Wilson's footnote.

in pursuit till he should meet Colonel Murray. Monson, like his kinsman the opponent of Warren Hastings, was personally brave, but without sagacity, stability, or prudence. He marched by the Mukandwára Pass to Chambal. But Murray, misled by false information, by fear, or by prudence, had already retired; and Monson heard with dismay that he was opposed to the whole of Holkar's forces. He had only two days' supplies, and Sindhia's general, who was with him, poured tales of terror into his ears. Both Murray and Monson, wrote Arthur Wellesley, pithily, 'seem to have been afraid of Holkar, and both to have fled from him in different directions.'

Monson turned to retreat. Holkar, whose 'fortune was on the saddle of his horse,' played about him with light cavalry, cutting off his stragglers, defeating and destroying his irregular horse, and depriving him of his supplies [1]. News reached Lake on the 18th inst. that the retreat had begun, but he did not appreciate the extent of the disaster. 'I think,' he wrote to Wellesley [2], 'Holkar will not easily get his cavalry to attack our infantry unless he brings his guns, which will retard him and prevent his horse from doing much mischief. His guns will, in the end, be the cause of his ruin. His insolence is admirable. . . . I trust he may yet get a very severe check from Colonel Monson.' But though he wrote

[1] Cf. Major Wm. Thorn, *Memoirs of the War in India*, 1805-6, pp. 357 et sqq; and the Diary of the Retreat, in *East India Military Calendar* ii. 538-559.

[2] July 21, 1804, *Wellesley Despatches*, iv. 178.

in this strain it is evident that Lake saw that the affair was serious, and he must bear the blame of taking no immediate steps to assist the retreating force. The conclusion of his letter is curious as illustrating the warmth of personal feeling between the Governor-General and his subordinates, and how keenly, it was known, Wellesley felt with and for his forces in the field :—

'I write in great haste and have only to beg you will not suffer this late unpleasant business to affect you, but will believe that everything shall be done to correct the evil, which is certainly not agreeable. Despondency will be of no avail, we must therefore set to work and retrieve our misfortune as quick as possible (sic). I feel myself quite well and able, if necessary, to encounter any fatigue of body and mind; of the latter, I am, like your Lordship, pretty well used to it. That I may live to see you enjoy peace of mind, health and happiness, is the sincere wish, my dear Lord, of your affectionate and devoted servant.— G. LAKE.'

But disaster followed disaster. Zalím Singh of Kotah (whom Lake in the same letter believed to have acted remarkably well) refused to suffer the retreating troops to enter his land. The rains came on, and in pitiable condition, across swollen rivers and soft and impassable roads, the retreat was continued. Before long it became impossible to ford the rivers; boats had to be procured or rafts made, and the retreat became slower and more beset with attacks. Monson, too, showed little judgement. He received succours at Rámpura on July 29, when he should have turned on his foes with his whole force. But he was slow where he should have been quick, and hasty where he should have deliberated. He remained nearly a month at Rámpura, and at last resumed a retreat which soon became a flight. Finally Sindhia's troops deserted him: he was wofully cut up in every engagement: at last a disorderly rout streamed into Agra at the end of the month. 'I will not,' wrote Lake, when the account of all the disasters at last reached him, 'I will not at present say anything more upon this disgraceful and disastrous event . . . a finer detachment never marched. . . . I have lost five battalions and six companies, the flower of the army, and how they are to be replaced at this day, God only knows. I have to lament the loss of some of the finest young men and most promising in the army[1].'

It is not part of the scheme of this memoir to enter upon the details of military movements, and for this defeat it is clear that the Governor-General was in no way responsible. Arthur Wellesley, with his cool, clear judgement, soon analyzed the cause of the disaster[2]. 'I am decidedly of opinion,' he writes, 'that Monson advanced without reason and retreated in the same manner; and that he had no intelligence of what was passing five miles from his camp.' He wrote later, in a letter which became classical since

---

[1] Sept. 2, 1804, *Wellesley Despatches*, vol. iv. p. 197.

[2] There are several letters on the subject in *Selections from Wellington Despatches* (ed. Owen), pp. 430, 431.

Peel called it the finest military letter he had ever read:—

'In the first place, it appears that Colonel Monson's corps was never so strong as to be able to engage Holkar's army if that chief should collect it; at least the Colonel was of that opinion. Secondly, it appears that it had not any stock of provisions. Thirdly, that it depended for provisions upon certain Rájás who urged its advance. Fourthly, that no measures whatever were taken by British officers to collect provisions either at Búndi or Kotah, or even at Rámpura, a fort belonging to us in which we had a British garrison. Fifthly, that the detachment was advanced to such a distance, over so many impassable rivers and *nullahs*, without any boats collected or posted upon those rivers; and, in fact, that the detachment owes its safety to the Rájá of Kotah, who supplied them with his boats. The result of these facts is an opinion, in my mind, that the detachment must have been lost, even if Holkar had not attacked them with his infantry and artillery.'

The lessons for Indian warfare which Wellesley drew from the campaign are concise and valuable—and it may be that the disaster was a cause of prudence which brought later success. At any rate it was a lesson which native ballads long kept alive and which British officers did not soon forget.

The Governor-General showed no disposition to shirk responsibility—though he was in no way to blame. He generously said, 'Whatever may have been Monson's fate or whatever the result of his misfortunes to my own fame, I will endeavour to shield his character from obloquy, nor will I attempt the mean purpose of sacrificing his reputation to save mine[1].'

The disaster was fatal. It was, indeed, the final blow to Wellesley's position. The enthusiasm of the public and the thanks of the legislature, won by his glorious achievements, had only just held the balance against the Company's increasing irritation. This was the end of their hesitation. In terror they determined that he must return at once and his whole policy be reversed. Nor was the blow felt less in India. It aroused all the fire still lingering in the hearts of the Maráthás, it brought again Sindhia and Bhonsla to throw off the bonds of their English alliance, it encouraged all India to believe that, as Holkar could conquer them, the British were not invincible. But for Monson, Holkar would have been crushed in a few months, Wellesley's policy would have achieved complete and triumphant vindication, and the great problem of English relations with the Maráthás would not have waited for solution till 1818[2].

The reverse, however, was only momentary. Colonel Murray had already returned and seized Holkar's capital, Indore. Holkar himself laid siege to Delhi on October 8, and continued the siege till the 14th. The defence was as wise and heroic as Monson's retreat had been the reverse. A mere handful of

---

[1] *Wellesley Despatches*, vol. iv. p. 205.

[2] See *The Marquess of Hastings*, by Major Ross-of-Bladensburg, C.B., in this Series.

Sepoys, ably commanded by one who knew his men, defended that great city—ten miles in circumference—with brilliant success.

The enemy finally retired before Lake came up. Holkar now made an attempt to ravage the Company's territories, relying as he had hitherto done so successfully on the swiftness of his cavalry. He marched down the Doáb, pillaging and burning as he went. On November 12, the British troops under General Frazer found him entrenched at Díg: and on the next day attacked him. A brilliant victory was won, in which the gallant 76th, who had already covered themselves with glory during this war, carried all before them. Three days later General Lake destroyed a large body of Holkar's cavalry at Farukhábád. He then advanced to Díg and besieged the town and citadel, which he entered on December 24.

Lake, however, was destined himself to meet with reverses. He determined to punish the Rájá of Bhartpur, who had deserted the English for Holkar. The fortified town, more than six miles in circumference, well garrisoned and ably defended, resisted all the efforts of Lake, who, indeed, as Wellington said, 'blundered terribly' and lost over three thousand men in his fruitless assaults. Lake was a cavalry general, and had no knowledge of siege operations. He was more effectual in driving away Holkar's relieving force; and thus the Rájá of Bhartpur, in April, agreed to a treaty without the capture of his fortress.

The rest of the operations of the war are without interest. It is clear that but for political changes Holkar would have been completely conquered, and Wellesley, 'without renouncing any advantage, would have been able to effect every arrangement for securing a long, if not a permanent, tranquillity [1].'

But Wellesley's government was at an end. When the Directors heard of Monson's disaster they were terrified. His recall was hastened, and his successor, Lord Cornwallis, arrived in Calcutta on July 30, 1805. Wellesley knew that this meant the complete reversal of his policy—and the war was abandoned at the moment when success was at last assured.

The war with Holkar would probably have been considered a successful one had not Wellesley's previous achievements raised the standard of English expectations in Indian warfare. Holkar's power was so shattered as to be within measurable distance of extinction. His allies were utterly weakened or had deserted him. There was no Marátha power left strong enough to withstand the British. But the interval, during which Wellesley's policy was abandoned, revived all the old difficulties and left to Lord Hastings a task as hard as that on which Wellesley had engaged.

At the conclusion of an account of the military history of the great Governor-General some estimate of the wisdom of his territorial acquisitions may be expected. This, if one postulate be granted, can only

[1] Grant Duff, vol. iii. p. 303.

take the form of a vindication. Ought Great Britain to have conquered any Indian territory? If the action of her merchants and soldiers was justified, we cannot withhold, not only our pardon, but our admiration from Wellesley. While others had patched up hollow treaties and taken little tracts of country, which gave responsibility without affording the means of rightly exercising it, he for the first time had seen the breadth of the question that was before his countrymen. It was no matter of rupees or of individual greed or aggression. India craved for firm rule, for freedom from tyranny and corruption, for expansion and liberty. There was no power, Muhammadan or Hindu, which could fulfil these demands. The British Company stood already among them, and from it alone could union and regeneration spring. At home the Directors thought of commerce, the Government of policy; no one but Wellesley saw that there lay before us the making of an empire, and through that of a nation. He wrote to Castlereagh[1], when the Maráthá war was in prospect:—

'I cannot suppose that the condition of the Company, with relation to any part of its territorial possessions in India, can be considered to be similar to that of a private individual proprietor of a landed estate. The Company, with relation to its territory in India, must be viewed in the capacity of a sovereign. If any other principle be recognised and the Company be permitted to hold the nominal sove-

[1] *Wellesley Despatches*, vol. iii. pp. 153 sqq.

reignty of India, endless confusion must ensue; in such an extremity no possible remedy could save this country from anarchy and ruin but the instantaneous assumption of the direct executive power of the British possessions in India by the Crown of the United Kingdom.'

This was his greatness—that he recognised, in all their fullness, alike the need and the responsibility of the expansion of British India.

CHAPTER VI

GOVERNMENT, EDUCATION, AND DEFENCE

WELLESLEY was not one of those who use a machine without caring to understand its mechanism. He was, rather, like the workman who finds an engine to his hand which, while he employs all its powers to the best advantage, he sees to be capable of important improvements, and sets himself, in the light of his own experience, at once to remedy and to perfect. And here two points especially demand notice. The first is Wellesley's account of the system as he found it, the second the designs which he entertained for its improvement.

In an elaborate minute of July 9, 1800[1], the Governor-General in Council described the state of the Government as it was. The Governor-General in Council possessed supreme executive power, exclusive legislative authority, and 'as constituting the Courts of Sadr Diwání Adálat and the Nizámat, or the chief civil and criminal courts, the Governor-General in Council also exercises a large portion of the judicial power.' The original aim of the framers

[1] *Wellesley Despatches*, vol. ii. pp. 312 sqq.

of this system of Government was to model it on principles drawn from the British constitution; and this, with the necessary modifications, had been accomplished. In some points the arrangements had been highly satisfactory. 'The reasons which originally occasioned the continuance of the entire legislative and executive authority in the Governor-General in Council are obviously of a permanent nature.' But it was beyond the power of the Governor-General in Council adequately to perform the judicial duties, and the union of judicial and legislative functions in the same body was also contrary to the 'general and established principles of government.' The security of private rights should be absolutely independent of those in political office, nor should officers of state have power to render the laws nugatory by abuses, omissions, or delays in their administration. Great inconvenience also arose from the fact that the proceedings in these high courts, as they were then constituted, must always be heard *in camerâ*, and without the presence either of the parties or their pleaders. In consequence of these evils the Governor-General in Council now determined to reconstitute these two high courts, giving each the same body of distinct judges, with the full power at present enjoyed by the Governor-General and the members of Council, who were in future no longer to constitute the Courts.

The minute then gives a description of the executive duties of the Governor-General in Council. These included the management of all foreign relations, and, in internal government, the management of the public revenue, the superintendence of the general finance of India, the regulation of the army, and much miscellaneous business. Besides these and other duties of executive control—the most important being exercised in relation to the Presidencies of Madras and Bombay—the Governor-General had the superintendence of the Company's commercial concerns. The duties involved the employment of a number of important officials, and it was absolutely essential that these should be 'men of the first talents and ability.'

This sketch of the powers and duties of the Governor-General led naturally to two inferences; first, that especially in view of the Governor-General's authority over the other Presidencies, some modification or rearrangement would be beneficial; and second, that the utmost care should be taken in the selection and training of the Company's officers. It is on this second point alone that Wellesley dwells in the minute of July, 1800; and to this we will return. On the first point we have little published material from which to infer the opinions of the great statesman. There exists, however, happily, in the Record Department of the India Office, a paper [1] containing his plan for the improvement of Indian Government, which is of the greatest interest. Its value is increased by the manuscript notes of Dundas which are attached to it. In this minute Wellesley suggests the Union of the Governments of Bombay and Ceylon

---

[1] Fisher Papers, 306 (2207).

under the Presidency of Madras. The whole of the British possessions in India should then be governed by a Governor-General, and two Councils, with a Vice-President to each. The Governor-General would change his residence from time to time, and would control every part of the detail in both presidencies. The Vice-Presidents should have full power in the absence of the Governor-General, except that all patronage ought to be subject to his control. They should always be appointed from England; and neither of them should ever hold the office of Commander-in-Chief. The Governor-General should always have a direct commission from the Crown. This is of the first necessity, because it is urgent that he should be able to exercise authority, ultimate and final, over both Army and Navy.

There was also a defect in the Governor-General's legislative powers. He had no right, for instance, to impose any tax on articles of consumption at Calcutta, which should be part of his legislative function. Finally, Wellesley alludes to a matter which was a personal annoyance to himself, the legal necessity for the presence of the Governor-General at every Council meeting. The senior member present, he suggests, should preside in his absence, but no act should be valid without his signature. Of the Governor-General himself, Wellesley writes, characteristically enough, that he should 'always be a peer of Great Britain, it being absolutely necessary to the maintenance of his authority in India that he should be a person of high rank. He should also be a person, if not conversant in Indian affairs (which is the most desirable), at least well accustomed to public business.'

The interest of those suggestions is considerable, and scarcely less interesting are the comments of Dundas, since they may be taken to show why the proposals of Wellesley were not brought forward in any public way. Dundas thought that, with the exception of the union of the presidencies of Madras and Bombay, there was no pressing reason for change. It would not be proper to give the Governor-General a commission or authority over the king's forces, nor could anything be done in the matter of the navy. Legislative defects should be remedied, for it is essential 'that the legislative authority should be exercised on the spot, and by every means the detail of it kept out of the British Parliament.' Dundas was evidently not enthusiastic in the matter; his comments are the familiar ministerial reply 'the subject shall receive the most careful attention.'

We have other criticisms of the project, and it is evident that it was seriously considered. Mr. Bragg, writing on April 16, 1800[1], gives his opinion on some of the proposals, particularly on that for uniting the subordinate presidencies. It could be done, he says, by Act of Parliament abolishing the Bombay presidency and vesting its powers in Madras. It would be expedient to transfer the seat of government to Seringapatam—a curious suggestion, showing how

[1] India Office MSS., Fisher Papers, 308 (2209).

greatly the centre of interest had shifted, through Wellesley's policy, from the West to the South.

Nothing came, for the present at least, of any of the suggestions. There is no date to the copy of the minute in the India Office; but it must be earlier than 1800, so that it cannot be said to be based on Wellesley's maturest experience. It expresses, however, with great clearness the views of which his published correspondence contains many a hint—that the powers of the Governor-General were inadequately defined and unsatisfactorily exercised, and that his control over the subordinate presidencies ought to be greatly strengthened and enlarged. To Wellesley, it is unquestionable, the ideal of Indian Government was an 'imperial theme': the responsibility was so vast, the interests were so widespread, the destinies of the rule so uncertain, that divided control was intolerable. The ruler of British India, to his mind, must be implicitly trusted; and he must be practically absolute. Laws laid down for him as fundamental he would follow; but policy he must dictate, and it must be his to deal, unchecked, with the exigencies of the moment. Wellesley chafed at the narrow, petty, tradesmanlike opinions of the Company; he would be, as he was, the Architect of Empire. But it cannot be forgotten that though magnificent as a master he must have been to the last degree exasperating as a servant. He was not trained to go in harness. Yet however autocratic he would have made himself, however extended might be the power which he would have conferred on the Governor-General, it was not power so much as efficiency that he sought. And this is to be seen in his pursuit of the object which was, after all, probably the nearest of all his projects to his heart, and which, in the eyes of posterity, perhaps most clearly marks him as a man of liberal and prescient wisdom. If he would magnify the office he would educate the officials. His despatch of July 9, 1800, ends with an appeal on behalf of a more complete and definite training of the Company's servants. Minute after minute exists on this subject, and the records of the India Office and the British Museum are full of papers to develope and illustrate it.

On October 24, 1799, writing to Dundas [1], Wellesley in brief explained the cause and the aim. 'The state of the administration of justice, and even of the collection of revenue throughout the provinces, affords a painful example of the inefficacy of the best code of laws to secure the happiness of the people, unless due provision has been made to ensure a proper supply of men qualified to administer these laws in their different branches and departments.' The Company's writers arrived in India ignorant, and lived there without control. Discipline, and education, these they wofully lacked, and these it should be the Company's duty, as it was the

[1] *Wellesley Despatches*, vol. ii. pp. 131-2.

Governor-General's own determination, in some measure to supply.

It may be doubted if, in our days of propriety and competition, we have at all realized the condition of the Indian civilians of the last century. A few brilliant novels, some sober biographies of great and impeccable personages—these are the materials on which our conceptions are formed. But these treat rather of the men who rose to fame, of the strenuous and hardy workers who will be found under all conditions of life, and who will thrive in any atmosphere however unwholesome. And again, their picture of Anglo-Indian society, though it dwells with freedom on the humorous and the *bizarre* at Calcutta or Bombay, does not lift the veil which hangs over the life of the official in distant outposts, where he went a boy in his teens, with hot passions and no shred of external control over his personal affairs, as the only representative alike of Western civilization and the dominion of a conquering and despotic race. There are memories of old Calcutta vile enough to suggest how much worse may have been the conditions under which men lived where there was no semblance of English society, and no social code however imperfect and athwart.

In spite of the many noble and honourable names which dignify the Company's service, was not the English conception of an Anglo-Indian official drawn from a class whose habits were at once ludicrous and corrupt? The figure which a returned civilian cuts in the literature of the early part of our own century suggests a very different training from that which has given us the stern self-suppression and devotion to duty, the philanthropy and the zeal, of our day.

Wellesley says simply enough that 'sloth, indolence, low debauchery, and vulgarity' are 'too apt to grow on those young men who have been sent at an early age into the interior part of the country, and have laid the foundations of their life and manners among the coarse vices and indulgences of those countries.'

Such were the admitted evils. In his 'Notes with respect to the Foundation of a College at Fort William[1],' Wellesley explained in detail the educational defects which appeared to him to be notorious. In the early days of the Company the duties of its servants were exclusively commercial, but with the growth of its territorial power they had become charged with the conduct of intricate negotiations, the management of complicated systems of revenue and finance, and the dispensing of justice over millions of people of various languages, manners, and creeds. The civil servants of the Company were no longer agents of a commercial concern, they were in fact the ministers and officers of a powerful sovereign. From merchants they had become statesmen, from traders magistrates, ambassadors, governors, and judges. For these manifold duties it was no more than decent that their training should be strict and their education serious. 'Finally, their early habits should be so formed as to

[1] July 10, 1800, *Wellesley Despatches*, vol. ii. pp. 325 sqq.

establish in their minds such solid foundations of industry, prudence, integrity, and religion, as should effectually guard them against those temptations and corruptions with which the nature of this climate, and the peculiar depravity of the people of India, will surround and assail them in every station.'

That the present system of education was inadequate was a fact that needed no proof. The writers arrived in India, at the age of sixteen or eighteen, absolutely ignorant of their duties, and innocent of a trace of knowledge of the history, jurisprudence, ethics, and even the languages of the peoples whom they would be called to rule. Such education as they obtained at home was almost invariably narrow and commercial, and their studies entirely ceased at an age when they might have been most fruitfully developed. When they arrived in India their incompetence often led to indolence; nor was there any encouragement to continue their studies.

The remedy, says Wellesley, lies in a vastly improved education, of which the foundation must be judiciously laid in England and the superstructure systematically completed in India. The question then arises, in what proportion is the time of education to be spent in England and in India? Here Wellesley was the first to touch upon difficulties which can scarcely be said to be solved even by the latest changes of the Civil Service examinations. Is it possible for most parents to afford a long education in England? Can the necessary teaching be provided? Would not the delay in the civilian's time of going out cause many of the civil servants 'to form habits and connections at home not to be relinquished at that period of life without great reluctance?' If they went out older would they have a fair chance of returning to England with an independent fortune?

These were Wellesley's questions. Some of them have been answered; some appear to us now to need no answer; some recur in different forms. Wellesley's plan was at least the result of a candid and practical consideration of each of them. To him it appeared that a college in India was an essential feature of a satisfactory education for Indian Civil Servants. It seemed clear, for instance, that no better than a theoretical acquaintance with language, law, or custom could be obtained in England. To support this opinion there was the somewhat ludicrous example of Sir William Jones, renowned throughout Europe as an Orientalist, who was quite unintelligible at Calcutta to any native in any Eastern tongue.

A college, then, should be founded at Fort William. It would give opportunities for intercourse with learned natives. It would greatly encourage native teachers. As to the matter of cost, which he knew from the first would be the stumbling-block, Wellesley stated that, though endowment would be desirable, the Company need have no additional expense unless they approved, for the cost could be defrayed by a small contribution from all the Civil Servants in

India, to be deducted from their salaries. Such was his memorable despatch. He little expected the rebuff he received.

Meanwhile the College was founded, its regulations being drawn up by the Governor-General himself. The course of instruction sketched was wholly admirable. The regulations for discipline, residence, and government were modelled as far as possible upon those of the English Universities. Thus the College was established, and the course of instruction commenced. The Governor-General attended in state on great days, and distributed prizes, and addressed the students in his grandiloquent rhetoric. The results were highly satisfactory; and many of the first students who won distinction became eminent in the Company's service. Wellesley may have thought that success as well as necessity would justify the foundation. This was not the view of the Directors. With the utmost haste, and in utter disregard of the opinions of those best qualified to judge, they ordered the immediate abolition of the College. The blow was severe, and Wellesley felt it acutely. He addressed a long and on the whole temperate representation to the Court, which was unanimously supported by his Council: and he suspended the abolition till December 31, 1803.

He did not lack the approval of those entitled to judge of his scheme. One of the most powerful, as it is certainly among the most interesting of the representations made on its behalf, was that of the veteran Warren Hastings. Among the records in the India Office is a paper entitled ' Mr. Hastings's observations on Lord Wellesley's minute relative to the College at Fort William[1].' It is written in entire agreement with the scheme; and the more interesting passages will well bear quotation :—

'About thirty-five years ago,' he writes, 'I drew up a proposal for the establishment of a professorship of the Persian language in the University of Oxford, and presented printed copies of it to all the gentlemen who had at that time the direction of the Company's affairs. It had the approbation of the noble Lord who was then Chancellor of the University. The late Dr. Johnson promised, if it took place, to frame a code of regulations for the conduct of it. It met with no encouragement, and therefore dropped. In alluding to this circumstance I wish to have it inferred that what I have written upon the present subject is not the desultory suggestion of the moment, but the result of long and deliberative reflection; nor can I offer a more convincing proof of my entire agreement with Lord Wellesley in the object of his plan, than by thus making it appear to have been so long ago equally my own in principle though the means we severally proposed were different. I recommended that the writers of the Company after having received their appointment to this service, should be permitted to stay a competent time to prosecute and complete their studies in the branches of European learning, adding to them that of the Persian language in the University of Oxford. His Lordship has proposed the same process upon an enlarged scale, and to make Bengal the site of it. This is certainly preferable, as it will give the pupils the advantage of arriving in the

[1] Fisher Papers, 170 (1014).

country at a time of life in which the mind more easily conforms to the restraints of authority, the necessities of the climate, and the modes of society, than at a more advanced period. The languages, especially those that are of common use, are soonest acquired in the season of early youth; the organs being then most pliant to moderate themselves to their pronunciation and the understanding to catch and retain their ideas.'

The opinion of the Nestor of Indian administration cannot fail to have had great weight. With reluctance the Directors yielded to the powerful representations that were made to them by their own servants and by the Ministry, and permitted the maintenance of the College in a modified form for the benefit of the Bengal writers only, and solely for their instruction in Oriental languages. Thus Wellesley's scheme of a liberal education was nipped in the bud: but it at least succeeded in directing public attention to a crying scandal and a pressing need. It caused the foundation, a few years later, of the East Indian College at Haileybury, which for a time did admirable and most beneficial work. And though it was never carried out in its entirety it remained as a striking memorial of the width and wisdom of its framer's ideas, and may be looked back to as the foundation of all genuine training for one of the highest professions a British subject can undertake.

It is impossible in reading Wellesley's many papers on the training of civilians to avoid being struck by the stress he laid on the religious as well as the intellectual aspects of the question. The neglect of Christian duties, the ignorance of Christian doctrines[1], are constantly referred to as being associated with the low tone which marked the Indian services. At the head of the new College at Fort William he placed a Provost, and in his statutes for the institution he ordered that 'The Provost shall always be a clergyman of the Church of England[2].' He directed that 'The primary duties of the Provost shall be to receive the junior civil servants on their first arrival at Fort William, to superintend and regulate their general morals and conduct, to assist them with his advice and admonition, and confirm them in the principles of the Christian religion, according to the doctrine, discipline, and rites of the Church of England.'

This was merely an example of what was with him a reasoned and deliberate policy. He felt the disgrace inflicted upon the English name by the neglect which had fallen on the observance of Christianity. He determined that as far as was possible he would wipe away the reproach. Thus he marked the Conquest of Mysore by a day of solemn thanksgiving. On February 6, 1800, the Governor-General, the Chief Justice, the Commander-in-Chief (Sir Alured Clarke), the Members of Council, the Judges, and the public officers, civil and military, proceeded on foot to the New Church at Calcutta. The streets were

[1] *Wellesley Despatches*, vol. iv. p. 346.
[2] Ibid., p. 357.

lined with troops, and royal salutes were fired during the procession and at the *Te Deum*. It was the first occasion on which any national recognition of Religion had taken place: and it was marked by all the pomp and solemn dignity which the Governor-General could give it. Lord Wellesley was the first ruler of India to stand forth decisively as a Christian.

His interest was not merely ceremonial. He prohibited the sacrificial exposition of children in the Ganges and prepared by an investigation for the abolition of *Sati* by Lord William Bentinck. He made distinct efforts for the dissemination of Christianity; he caused the translation of the Bible into Bengalí, Hindustáni, Maráthí, Tamil, Persian, Chinese, and Malay; he seriously endeavoured to bring the ecclesiastical establishment of the Company into relation to the needs of their servants, and favoured the too long and shamefully delayed appointment of a Bishop. At the same time no one could more clearly express disapproval of secular endeavours to enforce Christianity. A strong letter of April 6, 1804, to the Governor of Ceylon, expresses with unquestionable wisdom the lines on which it was incumbent on a British Government to act, giving complete and unfettered toleration to all religions of the land. In him, for the first time, English and natives alike saw a ruler who did not leave the profession of his faith altogether out of count in his public policy, or justify the sarcasm of Burke that Englishmen were unbaptized during their voyage to India. When the proposals for the increase of the Church Establishment came before Parliament in 1813, he reviewed his own conduct with dignity and pride. He 'thought that a Christian Governor could not have done less, and knew that a British Governor ought not to do more.'

As Lord Wellesley was the first British ruler seriously to consider the questions of education and religion, so he was the first to definitely design a system of defence for the Empire which the Company had now come to rule. His defensive measures fall naturally under two divisions—those which form part of his external policy and those which are related to the internal administration.

In theory, and still with some amount of practical truth, the British power, like all other powers in India, owed respect if not homage to the Imperial name [1]. The Mughal Shāh 'Alám, so long the servant of Sindhia, the most aspiring and powerful of the Maráthás, was the only representative of an universal power that still lingered in the land. To him every prince professed obedience, and from him alone all dignities flowed; the greatest sovereigns of the land, with whom the English warred and treated as independent rulers, were merely his officers. Sentiment and the force of custom gave him, even in his degradation, an appreciable force in the political movements of the age. All was still done in his name: his sanction conferred on others the power which he could not wield himself.

[1] See *Sindhia* (by H. G. Keene) in this Series.

It was not until the Maráthá war that Wellesley was brought into immediate relations with the unhappy prince, who still lived, blinded and old, under Maráthá influence and guarded by the force of Perron and Bourquin, at Delhi. In July, 1803, the Governor-General sent instructions to General Lake to obtain constant information as to the condition of affairs at Delhi, and when that city should, in the course of the war, be occupied by the British troops, to pay to the aged monarch every attention, respect and reverence which should assure him of the Company's consideration and support. Writing to the Secret Committee a year later he dwelt upon the danger of allowing the French to re-establish their footing—as it seemed probable they might—under the shadow of the Imperial pretensions, and he urged the importance of placing Sháh 'Alám at once under British protection. When the defeat and surrender of Bourquin placed Delhi in the hands of Lake, the Mughal was treated with every consideration, and, by an arrangement notified to the Company on June 2, 1805, he was established, with substantial provision for his dignity and comfort, under British protection. This recognition (though somewhat tardy perhaps) of the importance of the Mughal name may be regarded as a measure of defence for the whole dominion of the Company, by connecting it in terms of alliance and protection with the one authority which had claim to recognition throughout India.

Relations with the great powers of the East must

form an essential part of any scheme of defence for our Indian Empire. Wellesley followed up his policy in Oudh and strengthened his position against Zemán Sháh by entering into alliance with Persia.

As early as February, 1799, he stated his views on the subject to the Governor of Bombay, and six months later he sent Captain Malcolm, whose ability and knowledge he had already recognised, as a special envoy to Teheran. The mission was entirely successful: a political alliance was formed which not only served to divert Zemán Sháh by an attack on his territory, but also secured to England an ally against France and Russia in the event of the invasion which the Czar Paul I was known to contemplate. A commercial treaty, by which the Persian ports were opened to the settlement and trade of British merchants, was also of considerable value. Wellesley wrote to the Directors: 'A firm and intimate connection has now been established between the British Government and a State, the resources of which are capable of aiding in an essential manner the hostile views of the enemies of the British nation against our Eastern possessions[1].' The relations thus begun were continued during Wellesley's Foreign Secretaryship (after his return to England) by the mission of Sir Gore Ouseley in 1811.

But it was not only from the North that invasion was feared. During the earlier part of Wellesley's administration there was considerable reason to believe

[1] *Wellesley Despatches*, vol. ii. p. 584.

that the French, if successful in Egypt, would attempt to recover their foothold in Southern India. Wellesley met this danger not merely by the war with Tipú and the treaties with the princes of the South, but by active intervention in the Egyptian campaign. In February, 1801, he sent an expedition to the Red Sea under the command of General Baird, and wrote to the Sherif of Mecca, the Imám of Senna, and the Sultán of Aden, calling upon them to join in expelling the French from the East. The expedition is interesting not for its results, which were trivial, but as showing the width of Wellesley's schemes, and the daring character of the statesman who, hedged by difficulties in the East, was not content with the defensive—for which an exhausted treasury might plead—or even with an active policy within the vast peninsula which he dominated, but took the offensive, and mingled in what was in reality an European war, by calling in the tributary East to redress the threatened balance of the West.

This movement was part, indeed, of a more extended policy. Wellesley had projects that included the Cape, the Isle of Bourbon, the Mauritius, the Philippine Islands, Ceylon. The Cape, he saw, was an 'outpost of India,' and he required it to assist not only in defence but in defiance. The naval force of the French islands inflicted a constant series of losses upon British trade. In February, 1801, Wellesley stated that British property worth over two millions had been carried into Port St. Louis since the beginning of the war. He planned the capture of the Mauritius, and would have placed the island in direct relation to the Indian defences. Everything here depended upon the swiftness of the action; and Admiral Rainier, a martinet of the most pedantic school, who had already, on another occasion, acted without Wellesley's orders in such a manner as seriously to embarrass his schemes, now refused to move without the express command of the King in the usual form. Wellesley's letter to the Admiral [1] is a masterpiece of indignant and sarcastic rhetoric. One passage will suffice for example:—

'If no advantage can ever be taken of the temporary or accidental weakness of the enemy's possessions in India, without express orders from England, signified through the usual official channels, not only to the Government of India but to the commanders of his Majesty's land and sea forces, it is evident that opportunities of reducing the enemy's power and resources must frequently be lost without the hope of recovery, by reference for formal commands to the source of sovereign authority at home. In the present instance an extraordinary and fortunate accident had disclosed to me the weak and almost defenceless state of the most important possessions remaining to France in this quarter of the globe. In my judgement I should have failed in my duty towards my king and country, if I had waited for his Majesty's express commands, or for his orders, signified through the official channels established by Parliament for the government of India, before I had proceeded to take the necessary steps for availing myself of the critical posture

[1] The correspondence is printed in *Wellesley Despatches*, ii App. Q.

of the French interests within the reach of the force entrusted to my control. The arduous powers vested in me by Parliament are sufficient to render my opinion in India a substitute for the occasional and unavoidable defect of precise and express commands from the sovereign authority of the British Empire.

'In the exercise of this discretion I am subject to a severe responsibility; but wherever it appears to me to be my duty to exercise my discretion and to apply for the assistance of his Majesty's naval force in the prosecution of my endeavours against the common enemy, I conceive that his Majesty's naval commander is not only justified in complying with my application but absolutely required to aid me, unless the condition of his ships shall preclude their co-operation, or unless, in his conscientious judgement, the attempt which I propose may appear to be impracticable or dangerous to the public service. The want of his Majesty's express commands will never be received either by his Majesty, or by the public, as an admissible justification of the conduct of any public officer for declining to co-operate against the enemy in an attack which appears to be practicable and which promises advantage to the general cause.'

To this he adds the curt dictum 'If the principle which your Excellency has adopted had governed my conduct, the conquest of Mysore would not have been achieved.'

Foiled in a venture which had seemed to promise so favourably, Wellesley was still urgent and insistent on the necessity of securing Ceylon. He regarded it as the bulwark of India, and chafed at the divided control which again stood in the way of the full use of its resources. It was intolerable that here, again,

King and Company, Governor and Governor-General should be at odds. Nor was Mr. Frederick North, Governor of Ceylon (whose name sufficiently explains his appointment), the most sensible of men. In a terse and vigorous letter to Dundas (May 10, 1801) Wellesley argued strongly in favour of formally annexing the island to the Crown, and placing it definitely under the control of the central power at Calcutta. Two principles, he said, are essential to the permanent efficiency of our Indian government—that every part, continental or insular, should be subject to the general control of one undivided authority; and that the constitution of each part should be alike, and subordinate to the authority which the Crown alone could confer. Here again his wishes were disregarded. Ceylon was wholly removed from the authority of the Company on January 1, 1802. The difficulties (especially at a time of war within and without the island) were by this step increased rather than diminished; and in a letter to Lord Hobart (November 30, 1803) Wellesley recorded them with a new demand that the island should be placed under the control of the Governor-General.

Happily Wellesley was not always so hampered as in the cases we have last considered. Even in external policy he could occasionally act boldly and at once. By the peace of Amiens the French possessions in India were to be restored, and a fleet set out to take possession and to re-establish their military power. At a time when a large French force under M. Perron was in existence in the North of India, and when the utmost efforts had been directed for years to the complete banishment of French influence from the whole peninsula, it was intolerable to Wellesley that the settlement should again be legally established. He boldly decided to refuse the restoration of territory, and instructed Lord Clive to decline to surrender Pondicherry and the other forts until the arrival of further instructions. The French General did not venture on an attack. The fleet sailed back to Mauritius; and the renewal of war within six months justified the prescience of the Governor-General. His promptness also in the occupation of the Portuguese and Dutch settlements of Goa and Serampur was a characteristic incident in this policy of security by external action.

Wellesley also planned, with the aid of his brother Arthur and other chief officers, a more systematic military defence than had yet been designed. The pretensions of the English power in India were really out of all proportion to its military strength. Again and again a combination of enemies might have brought about disaster and even ruin. But fortune favoured the audacity of the ruler. He was not himself blind to the weakness of the position. He constantly demanded more men from home, more officers, more ordnance.

In January, 1800, General Stewart, than whom no man was better qualified to speak from experience, drew up a minute on the general question of the defence of India, which he submitted to Dundas on his return to England in the following year.

He dwelt first upon the absolute necessity of securing the coast line. Commerce had brought us to the land, and commerce alone was our true cause for remaining there. The allurements of conquest led us to the interior; but wisdom by no means accompanied each step. Near the sea our establishments were safer, our support more secure, our armies better provided. Danger within might after all be regarded as slight. 'From the great superiority which we possess in courage and science, our dangers from the nations of India will never probably be imminent.' But the tide of invasion from the North is checked, not ended. The way of Alexander still lies open, and the wild races of the North lack only a leader to pour again over the plains of Hindustán. France is a still more pressing danger. The French are more popular in India—and ever have been—than we. Frenchmen are always favourably received by the native princes. The court of the Nizám bore witness to the weight and power that they so easily acquired. By the instrument of force, and the agency of fear alone did we expel them from Haidarábád, and any opportunity to return there or elsewhere would at once be taken. From this general statement—that an external not an internal foe is to be feared—General Stewart passes to a detailed examination of the defences of the British dominions. Ceylon should be secured and strongly fortified. Bengal with its dangerous river and its strong fortress is safe on every side but the North. Fortifications on the frontiers are necessary, as the northern tribes are ignorant of the art of sieges. Madras must be protected by a strong force. But it is on the West that danger is more to be feared. There the sea-coast is largely in Marátha hands. That way commerce lies. And if the French were now to land in Surat, our trade would receive a fatal blow; if in Gujarát, and in alliance with the Maráthás, they would be even more formidable than in Bengal. The decision at which he arrives is the necessity for obtaining control of Gujarát, as a security against North and West alike, a new trading centre and a country easy to defend. This control, it may be added, was happily obtained in 1802, through a treaty with the Gáckwár won by the tact and firmness of Major Walker.

The North-West frontier had been an earlier object of Wellesley's care. In October, 1798, Sir James Craig, who had been employed in various missions, diplomatic and military, supplied a full report on the condition of that district in view of the danger of an invasion from the North. He represented Oudh as being entirely unfortified. 'Except Allahábád, which hardly yet deserves the name, there is not a single fortress or place of strength in the whole country.' In this condition of affairs an alliance with the Maráthás seemed essential to security: with their aid the northern frontier might be pushed forward, and mutual defence would be a guarantee of its safety. But still a force of twenty thousand men, besides the garrison of Allahábád, would be needed. Then alliance through the Maráthás with the Sikhs and Rájputs would strengthen our power and increase our security.

When we turn from schemes such as these to note the actual number of British troops in India at the time, we receive a shock of surprise. Doubtless few even of the higher officers were aware how miserably inadequate was our fighting power: happily our enemies were in ignorance still more complete. It is certain, from reports prepared for the Governor-General, that the European force under his command at no time exceeded 14,000 men of all arms[1]. And of the supplies and equipments of the troops, native and British, another letter of Sir James Craig gives a description which may be taken without demur to apply much more widely than to the district of which it made report. 'Our stores,' he says, 'are utterly incompetent to any forward move, such as I have ventured to suggest as justifiable if co-operation with the Maráthás can be purchased by it. Our proportion of musket ammunition is 120 rounds per man, and that for the small arms of the cavalry is 40; with this I most certainly would not venture to stir a step from the Ganges, and how we are to get up more, in the time in which I think it is probable that it may be requisite for us to do so, I know not. . . . For our artillery we have 300 rounds, but that

[1] *Wellesley Despatches*, vol. i. p. 303.

is, if possible, still less equal to what we ought to have, at least in a depôt, to which we could have a much more ready access than we have to Chunar or Allahábád. The latter should be our grand depôt in which should be lodged a quantity of stores of every species, equal to every possible emergency; while a field depôt, fed continually from it, should move successively from post to post as we advance, and be always at hand to renew our deficiencies. Upon the whole, do not, my Lord,' he concludes, 'consider it as presumption if I say that I feel a great deal more arrangement to be necessary than appears to me to occur to others as such. It is an easy thing to put the whole upon the issue of one battle, and unfortunately it is the mode which is attended with the least trouble.'

If this description should be, as it may well be, typical, it will not be felt that Wellesley exaggerated the needs of the British settlement when he wrote to Dundas on July 13, 1800. The letter is one of his most carefully written statements; practical, detailed, clear, and eminently characteristic of the mind which planned with such precision the methods and the means by which alone great successes could be assured. The necessities of conquest, he points out, require an increased military force; if danger from some quarters is diminished, still the territory to be defended has expanded. The number of British troops should always be proportionate to that of the native forces, the sepoys, and irregular cavalry. It had been unavoidably necessary to increase the Indian army. The British troops, on the other hand, had received the scantiest accessions, not sufficient indeed to fill the ranks thinned by war and sickness. The Madras regiments (King's troops) instead of being 1,200 strong were sunk to an average of 500 men fit for duty. It appeared that the whole number of the King's infantry was not over 11,000 men, the deficiencies amounting to over 8,000. With the Company's troops the total might rise to 14,000. But the average of sick was extremely high and the total number of Europeans ready for active service would not exceed 10,500. That this at that time was utterly inadequate for the defence of the whole territory of the Company needs no proof; nor can Wellesley be said to have exaggerated the needs of defence when he stated them at 30,000 men. The whole of this infantry should be King's troops. Again we have brought before us the importance of the undivided control of the Crown. The Company's troops, on the other hand, should be transferred as far as possible to the artillery, to fill some of the woful gaps in the ranks.

Dundas's reply, written six months later, illustrates most pointedly the obstacles against which the Indian rulers had to fight. Lack of money is the burden of it all—no money to pay troops or to discharge debts. To this he adds doubt of Wellesley's accuracy and denial of the needs of an expanded Empire. The strength of the enemy, not the extent of our possessions, should be the measure of our military force. There is much more, and in detail, in the same strain, all sensible and sound argument from the standpoint of the civilian and the banker. 'My present creed with regard to India is that nothing new is to be attempted without weighing well every rupee it will cost.' This was indeed attempting to govern great nations on the maxims of the counter. It was easy to write, at Wimbledon or Whitehall, that no aggression must be allowed. But the very life of the young Indian Empire—for Empire it had become—depended on its growth. This all Governor-Generals sooner or later were forced to recognise. The expansion could not be checked. Territory fell into their hands as ripe fruit falls from the tree when the winds blow. With means ridiculously inadequate there had been achievements beyond all hope. It was difficult enough to keep pace with the expansion, yet fatal —if it were possible—to lag behind.

But the Directors were blind to the military needs. They actually sent a peremptory order to reduce the military forces in India at the end of the year 1801 [1], a step so markedly condemnatory of the Governor-General's action that he dwelt upon it with peculiar feeling in his letter to Addington announcing his resignation. It was impossible to comply with the order without endangering the conquests that had already been made and entering upon the Marátha war with forces utterly inadequate. Wellesley there-

[1] *Wellesley Despatches*, vol. iii, Introduction.

fore suspended the orders of the Court; and the course of events made it impossible for them ever to be carried out. He gave bitter expression to his disgust:—

'The augmentation had been made under my express authority after the fullest deliberation and after consulting all the most experienced officers in India. The principle of these augmentations of the army is directly condemned by the Court. The increased force is stated to be unnecessary and to have been raised in an objectionable mode, and no option is left to my discretion with regard to the reduction enjoined. This order cannot admit of any other construction than that the Court of Directors has judged me to have been either ignorant of the force necessary for the preservation of the Empire founded in the Peninsula in the year 1799, or to have negligently or wickedly increased the army at Madras and Bombay without adequate necessity[1].'

It may be asserted that Wellesley greatly exaggerated the needs of our defensive establishment. But he had the assent of his temperate and keen-sighted brother, a man who estimated as no other English general did, alike the possibilities and the limits of what a small force could do. Arthur Wellesley wrote constantly on the subject, and returned to it long after he had left India. Writing, for instance, from Elvas in March, 1812, to Dundas, now Lord Melville, he expressed views similar to those held by his brother ten years before. The sum of his recommendations was that the European army in the East

[1] *Wellesley Despatches*, vol. iii. p. iv.

ought to be the King's, the Native army the Company's, so long as the Company should continue to be sovereign of the country. The Crown should name both Governor and Commander-in-Chief, as thus disputes between them would be less likely to arise. 'All authority, civil and military, must be vested by the law in the Governor in Council. The law must recognise no other authority in the State.' He adds significantly, 'the Directors must be prevented from meddling with or peddling in the discipline of the army. It is a matter of too serious consequence to be allowed to be jobbed at the India House.'

The persistency of Wellesley was, after all, not without results: and indeed the English ministers began to see the necessity for a largely increased force. Castlereagh, in 1804, wrote that he had always been anxious to increase the army, particularly the European army[1]. A considerable increase, indeed, was made, but not in the English troops. During Wellesley's rule the Bengal infantry was raised from twenty-eight to fifty-four battalions, the Bombay from twelve to eighteen, the Madras from thirty to fifty; with a proportionate increase in the Company's cavalry and artillery. While the English troops in India were largely increased, the Company's English infantry was practically dissolved, only one regiment remaining for each Presidency.

[1] India Office MSS. contain a volume of Castlereagh's Letters on the condition of the European Army, 1802-1805 (MS. List of Records, No. 3, 146, vol. 120).

Thus steps were taken towards the accomplishment of Wellesley's two chief aims, the increase of the army and its adequate control under one authority. But the great danger of a disproportionate number of Sepoys was left unheeded, until fifty years later Wellesley's warning was terribly enforced by the Mutiny.

CHAPTER VII

FINANCE: TRADE: QUARRELS WITH THE DIRECTORS

For the chief servant of a trading company the control of finance, it might seem, would be the main duty if not the main interest. But Wellesley, though a sound and sagacious man of business, was not a born financier. He possessed the power of choosing good instruments, of judging good work, of detecting flaws in a system submitted to him, which belongs to great men and which enables them to supervise with wisdom even where they cannot create with originality. Wellesley was a statesman first, then a soldier, diplomatist, financier. But in each of these fields he more than held his own with the ablest of his day.

At home the Company still felt itself to be mainly a great trading concern. Political interests and wider views of statesmanship and of empire were growing, very gradually, in the Court during Wellesley's administration; but to the last there was always—there could not fail to be—an eye to the dividends. The days were passed when with a

revenue of a million and a half there was a debt of
over three millions, while the Company paid twelve
and a half per cent. dividend and applied to Parliament to help them to keep it up. The Government
control and the renewed charter made the difference
between 1773 and 1798; but still the desire of the
shareholders was to be traders, not sovereigns. A
good income and a good opening for their sons and
kinsfolk—payment and patronage—these were the
points on which directors and proprietors fixed their
eager gaze. He was a good governor who made a
good dividend and found places for the scions of
comfortable stockholders: and he was a far way
towards the Court's displeasure who increased armaments, overran territory, and promoted on his own
choice.

Wellesley, immediately on his arrival in India, set
himself to obtain a clear view of the financial condition of the three Presidencies. In his minute of
June 12, 1798, he stated that he had determined to
revise all the public establishments, with the assistance of a committee, of which Mr. H. St. George
Tucker, a young Bengal civilian, was to be secretary.
The condition of affairs is thus summarised in Sir
Arthur Wellesley's memorandum:—

'The Company were found to have a revenue of £8,059,880,
a sum less than that which they had been found to have in
1793 at the renewal of their charter, by £165,748. The
debt amounted to £10,866,588, having increased since 1793;
and the interest was annually £746,933, having increased

since 1793. The total amount of the charges of the Government in India, including the interest of the debt, was £8,178,626; and the deficiency of the revenues, in comparison with the charges, at a time of profound peace, in India, was £322,530. At the same time the Company's credit was at the lowest ebb. Money could not be borrowed in Bengal at 12 per cent. interest; the Company's bonds and securities at that rate were circulated at such a discount, as well at that Presidency as at Madras and Bombay, as to amount to nearly a stagnation; and with this great war in expectation, the Company's financial servants were entirely at a loss to find the means for supporting and carrying on the ordinary operations of the government in time of peace [1].'

But the new Governor-General managed to inspire an entirely new spirit into the money market. 'Bankers and merchants,' says Mr. Torrens, 'took courage from the spectacle of an improved vigour in all branches of the administration, and lent the Government large sums of money where a few months before they would not discount Treasury Bills at less than usurious interest [2].' And the improvement thus begun continued, in spite of the enormous drains on the resources of the Empire, throughout the whole of Wellesley's rule. In their report of January 28, 1800 [3], the Governor-General and Council were able to announce that the state of public credit was more favourable than it had ever been during the preceding three years, 'the discount

---

[1] Owen, *Selections from Wellesley Despatches*, p. lxxiv.
[2] *Marquess Wellesley*, p. 180.
[3] *Wellesley Despatches*, ii. 185-193.

being this day on eight per cents. about five per cent., and on six per cents. about thirteen and a half per cent.' The Directors had sent a large quantity of bullion to India which had materially lightened the financial pressure and increased the feeling of security so essential to a prosperous conduct of mercantile operations. In March of the same year, Wellesley announced a steady improvement, showing progressive prosperity. The debt was becoming more manageable and the rate of interest was sinking. Government loans were much more readily taken up and on more favourable terms. The control of the finances was placed under Mr. Tucker, in whose hands the whole system was greatly improved and the terrors of the debt were greatly diminished. In July, 1803, Wellesley wrote to Castlereagh, when exaggerated fears had been expressed :—

'The proportion which the Indian debt now bears to our annual revenues, the reduction effected in the rate of interest upon public loans since the year 1798, the amount and operation of the sinking fund established in India, the present high credit of all securities of government, and the flourishing and progressive character of every branch of our resources must satisfy your lordship that exaggerated apprehensions have been disseminated with respect to the magnitude and pressure of the debt in India ; and that its existence cannot be considered to form the principal object of danger to India in a season of war with France.'

Again, in July, 1804, 'public credit continues to

[1] *Wellesley Despatches*, iii. 194.

improve' interest is being reduced and the debt is being discharged.

Mr. Tucker resigned his post in 1804, but not before he had elaborated a plan for the creation of a general Bank at Calcutta. In a letter of which a copy exists in the Fisher Papers at the India Office [1], he sketches both the provisional arrangements preparatory to its establishment, and the scheme on which it should be worked. He names as its chief advantages the issue of loans in specie at moderate interest to merchants who cannot get loans elsewhere save at exorbitant rates, and the issue of a smaller paper currency than that afforded by the Treasury Bills [2].

Connected with the question of finance was that of Private Trade [3]. The monopoly which the Company had guarded so jealously was restricted at the renewal of the Charter in 1793; 3,000 tons of freight were assigned to private traders. But it was clear that this would not suffice for the great increase of commerce. As a matter of fact the tonnage occupied with Bengal private goods reached over 6,000 tons in 1798–9, and over 7,000 in 1799–1800. The Company

[1] Fisher Papers, 205 (1390).

[2] An interesting account of the foundation of the Bank of Bengal, written by Mr. Tucker in 1838, will be found in the *Memoirs of Indian Government*, published from his papers, pp. 401 sqq.

[3] The chief documents on this subject are printed in a special supplement to vol. v. of the *Wellesley Despatches*. There are also in the India Office Miscellaneous Records, xxix, a mass of documents and memoranda, notes from Pitt, letters to and from Dundas, &c.

kept up its strong opposition to private trade in any form, whilst the Government endeavoured in a modified way to encourage it. Dundas, writing in 1797, pointed out to the London shipbuilders that already a great share of the produce of India was brought to England by other channels than those of the Company, and was brought to other ports than those of Great Britain, and that the encouragement of India-built ships would tell in favour of and not against British interests. As to the error of those who would prohibit the coming to England of India-built shipping, he wrote :—

'They conceive that the prohibition of India-built ships coming to Great Britain would make a proportionate degree of room for the shipping of the East India Company. It would have no such effect. It would have no other effect than that which it always has had, of driving those ships with their cargoes into foreign ports, and thereby establishing in foreign countries an Asiatic commerce founded on British capital, which by a contrary policy ought, in the first place, to centre in the River Thames and be from thence re-exported for the supply of other European nations. They are not aware of another essential point; such a prohibition would very rapidly injure the regular trade of the East India Company itself, for in consequence of the trade being carried on, to which I have last referred, foreign nations would be supplied with their assortments of Indian produce and manufacture, without having recourse for that purpose to Leadenhall Street, and in proportion as that mode of supplying themselves increased, exactly in the same proportion would the regular trade and the regular shipping in the

[1] *Wellesley Despatches*, v. 119.

employment of the East India Company decrease. The decrease of British shipping would not be the only consequence, the loss of commission and other consequences of British agency being employed in providing assortments for foreign countries, would also be withdrawn from the national capital.'

Wellesley, there seems reason to believe, was well read in Adam Smith, and his policy set, within the limited lines which his obligations to the Company allowed, in the direction of free trade. No one was bold enough to propose the abolition of the monopoly. Arthur Wellesley had already entered into the controversy on the subject. He accepted the quaint assertion, which appears to have been taken as an axiom by writers of the time, that it was entirely unwise to encourage free emigration of Englishmen to India, because the race would be deteriorated and the natives would by 'an unrestrained intercourse' lose their respect for the British name and character. But he declared that the Company's charge for freight, due to the cost of their expensive British ships, was so excessive that it discouraged trade, while at the same time the Company's own commerce was actually carried on at a loss. He still adhered to the principle of monopoly, and thought that the high duty on Indian sugar should be kept up, lest the West Indian islands should be annihilated. 'I conclude,' he wrote, 'that it is not advisable to throw open the trade, but that the Company ought to furnish private traders with the quantity of tonnage they might require at the lowest rate at which it could be got; that the import of Bengal articles ought to be as free for private traders as for the Company, and the export of British produce (military stores excepted) ought to be the same.'

But Dundas told the Directors in April, 1800, that 'two material circumstances attended the monopoly —first, that the exportable produce of India exceeds what at present the capital of the East India Company is capable of embracing; second, that the monopoly of the East India Company does not rest on principles of Colonial exclusion, for the trade to and from India is open to the subjects of other countries in unity with Great Britain.' Was then the remainder of Indian commerce, which the Company were unable to undertake, to be absorbed by foreigners or by British subjects? It was clear, both politically and commercially, that the latter should be preferred. And it was equally clear that the best method of transit was by India-built shipping. The clause in the Act of 1793, which restricted private trade to 3,000 tons, should be repealed, and British subjects in India should be freely allowed to bring home their funds in the shipping of the country. The fortunes and capital created in India should be transported in the manner most beneficial to the owners and to the nation, instead of being 'transferred through the medium of conveyance by foreigners and thereby adding to the wealth, capital, and navigation of foreign countries.'

These views were cordially accepted by Wellesley.

A letter of Mr. Udny, an eminent member of the Bengal Council, to the Governor-General, written probably at his own suggestion, showed a reason for welcoming an extension of liberty to British subjects in the rapidity and success of the commercial operations of the Americans.

'Under the present system of things the Americans bid fair to exclude us from the market for sugar in Europe . . . It is impossible that British merchants can, under the present order of things, cope successfully with such alert rivals. Every consideration of benefit to British individuals and of advantage to the British nation, calls for speedy measures of reform respecting the trade of India, to which the scarcity of English shipping available here this season seems now more particularly to invite.'

Everything was tending in the direction of free trade; but the tendency was slow, and the Directors still bitterly opposed concession. They appealed to the legislative monopoly, formally renewed for twenty years in 1793, and one of them actually used the argument that free trade with India would depopulate Great Britain. 'The second point which I strongly hold,' wrote Mr. Grant, 'is that an unlimited intercourse between Great Britain and India, such as subsists between Britain and her American colonies, would thin this country of inhabitants and fill our Eastern possessions with eager adventurers, even from all parts of Europe, who would vex, harass, and perplex the weak natives, and finally endanger if not occasion the overthrow of our dominions in the East.' 'Free trade,' cried the Company, 'cannot be permitted without being followed by a general intercourse, nor that without hazard to our political power in the East.'

It is needless to say that such absurd speculations did not enter the sober brain of Wellesley himself. The clearest expression of his policy is to be found in a letter to the Court of Directors, dated September 30, 1800. The employment of India-built ships was no longer a matter of expediency but of necessity, in order to convey the Company's own articles to Europe. He therefore adopted the plan of hiring ships on behalf of the Company, and reletting them to the proprietors of ships; leaving the proprietors of ships and the merchants at liberty to settle the terms of freight. He had no doubt that if British merchants in India were permitted to provide their own tonnage as they needed it, they would soon acquire the whole of the private export trade from India to Europe, and would render London the universal mart for the produce of Asia. The expansion of private trade would be an enormous benefit to India and to England. Only the surplus which the Company could not control would be absorbed in this way; for the Company would never be assailed in its most important articles of investment, piece goods and raw silk, for the long-standing position in India and the exceptional privileges granted by different states, as well as the restriction on all trades by means of licences, would

[1] Letter given in *Wellesley Despatches*, vol. v. p. 136.

preserve its supremacy in all that was essential to its commerce. Wellesley's views were supported by Castlereagh and Dundas, and the mercantile interest in England was wholly in his favour. But the bitterness of the Company and of the British ship-builders was in no way mollified. Here, then, in another point which they deemed vital, the Directors were at variance with their Governor-General.

The quarrel was not confined to matters of magnitude, to imperial policy or commercial freedom. The peddling interests of patronage and penuriousness were at stake.

The patronage of the Governor-General was a point which such a man as Wellesley would naturally regard as essential to his dignity and authority. Proud and self-contained, he delighted in responsibility. He was a keen and just judge of men, absolutely and unswervingly honourable, scorning the faintest suspicion of favouritism or influence. It is clear from many passages in his correspondence that he regarded the patronage in his hands, with an almost strained scrupulousness, as a trust of the most sacred kind and of the most far-reaching consequence. He resented like a blow the control which the Directors from time to time asserted. Here more than anywhere he felt the difference of standpoint from which he and they regarded their duties and their connection. Personal interest never swayed the balance of his judgement by an hair's breadth; but with men at home, who had no personal contact with the dangers and responsibilities of the East, it was only too clear that private and family claims would weigh heavily.

The patronage in the hands of the Governor-General made him the recipient of a number of curious and instructive letters, which Wellesley appears to have preserved with a sardonic thought of their future publication. Dundas, who tried his best to colonize India with Scotsmen, was not slow in making known his wishes to the Governor-General. There was Mr. Graeme, whose 'father is a friend of Sir H. Mildmay, and is a member of the corporation of Winchester, which place Sir H. intends to represent in the next Parliament,' or Mr. George Suttie, who 'is connected with several of my family by blood,' and whose father, Sir George Suttie, ' was long a steady political friend of mine in Parliament,' to be supported—and many another from Lord Castlereagh or through personal friends. But to all these there was but one answer; and it came to be universally recognised—as Sir John Macpherson (who had himself been Governor-General) wrote—that ' merit and capacity to serve' were the only recommendations to which Wellesley paid attention. Even the First Gentleman in Europe, who had not blushed to solicit the interest of the incorruptible Cornwallis, did not venture to make any application to Wellesley. The sagacity of the Governor-General was as great as his impartiality; even Mr. Mill admits that he has seldom been surpassed in the skill with which he made choice of his instruments.

It was thus with a poignant disgust that Wellesley found the Directors insinuating suspicion of his appointments, censuring or rescinding them, and appointing men from England of inferior talents and untried capacity. They ordered the reduction of Arthur Wellesley's allowance during his command in Mysore. The Governor-General regarded this, not unnaturally, as 'the most direct, marked and disgusting indignity that could be devised.' They revoked the appointment of Colonel Kirkpatrick as political Secretary on grounds which were contradictory to their own past action. They ordered a gentleman, superannuated from another post, and inefficient for the duties, to be appointed acting President of the Board of Trade, thus passing over men alike his superiors and his seniors. But the most flagrant instance of all was the removal of the most eminent Madras civilian, Mr. Webbe, chief Secretary to Lord Clive, a man whose knowledge, probity, and sound judgement were renowned throughout British India. Mr. Webbe, wrote Wellesley bitterly, 'is not removed on account of any deficiency of talents, knowledge, assiduity or integrity, or on account of any excess of his power; but merely because he possesses a large share of the confidence of the Governor of Fort St. George, and because he adds to that crime the accumulated guilt of possessing an equal share of the confidence, respect, and esteem of the Governor-General.'

Beside such differences as these, minor matters pale:

but it was with no feeling of submission that Lord Wellesley learnt that his own personal expenses were keenly criticized. The new Government House which he caused to be built at Calcutta seemed to him a necessary expression of the dignity and magnificence of the great power now founded in the East. To the Directors it was an extravagance and a scandal. They caused minute enquiries to be made as to its cost, counted up the figures with penurious apprehension, wrote minutes and papers on it, and complained that 'the Court had received no direct information [1].'

As a matter of fact the Court was always hesitating between a desire to recall so insubordinate a Governor and a feeling that it would be impossible adequately to replace a man of genius. The Oudh affairs, the appointment of Henry Wellesley, the College at Fort William, the Bassein treaty, the Marátha war, the question of Private Trade, the expenses of the Government—these perpetually urged them to be rid of their too powerful servant. In the mass of documents at the India Office there are hundreds of papers of charges against him on every kind of score. There may be mentioned as an example a paper of twenty-three pages of *Instances wherein the Marquis Wellesley has not acted agreeable* (sic) *to the Court's Orders or the general rules of the Service* [2], in which the points chiefly dwelt upon

---

[1] See Fisher Papers, India Office MSS., 302 (2186).
[2] Ibid., 303 (2187).

are the acting without communication with the Court, not obeying their orders, appointing military officers to civil and diplomatic appointments, appointing to the same persons not in the Company's service, and the granting of large salaries and pensions. The cases of the College and of the appointment of Henry Wellesley are mentioned, and three papers dated April, 1804, are added on the negotiations at Poona in 1800, 'carried on without reference to the Court.' There is also a more elaborate *Narrative of the Acts of Lord Wellesley during his Government* [1], under the following heads: (1) Infraction of the constitutional authority and rights of the Council: (2) Acting in the greatest affairs without the previous sanction of the Government at home, when it might have been waited for; (3) Assumption of illegal powers; (4) Extending the controlling powers of the Supreme Government over the Presidencies to all the details of these Governments; (5) Illegal appointments and evasions of the law. These are charges which we might expect to be made against a Governor who both felt his responsibilities and magnified his office. That any illegal or even unconstitutional act was committed by Wellesley is certainly not proven, and is improbable in the light of his general character.

The cases of the delegation of powers in 1803 to General Wellesley and General Stewart were sub-

---

[1] Fisher Papers, 301 (2183). The details are interesting, but the Paper is too long for analysis here.

mitted to counsel's opinion, and were, it is true, declared illegal by Mr. Ryder and Mr. Adam. But even they displayed some timidity in approaching the political question, and it is doubtful if a lawyer to-day would uphold their judgement. But that Wellesley took a large liberty of action in cases of urgency would not be denied, and indeed would probably have been claimed by himself as the foundation and the necessary condition of his greatness. It was the irony of his position that a man born to command should be shackled by the anile pedantry and timorousness of Leadenhall Street. As an Oriental despot he might have conquered a continent and gone down to posterity with Nadir Sháh or with Peter the Great. As the servant of a mercantile Company he could only walk in fetters and pine that he was not born to set right a disjointed time.

On January 1, 1802, he wrote to the Court, sending in his resignation. A letter (already quoted) to his friend Addington, who was then Prime Minister, went fully into the reasons for this step. Lord Clive had already been driven to retire, and Wellesley felt, in the face of conduct which he describes as 'highly offensive and disgusting to every sentiment of his mind,' that it would be impossible for him to retain his office 'with any prospect of private honour or of public advantage.' He repeated this request to be allowed to retire in a letter of March 13. The Directors were alarmed. Much had been begun which no one but Wellesley could complete. They desired him to remain in office till January, 1804, expressing in the strongest terms their conviction that the interests of the Company would be 'essentially promoted' by his continuance in India for another year, and they 'remained,' with that curious phrase of exuberant but formal cordiality which still survives in the official letters written by the Chancellor of the University of Oxford, his 'affectionate friends,' John Roberts, Jacob Bosanquet, and the rest.

Wellesley had told Addington that if the Ministry would assure him of their confidence and of their intention to afford him full support and protection he would remain in India till January, 1804 [1]. The Prime Minister wrote a cordial reply, and the Governor-General consented to remain. But he was still exposed to criticism which he could ill brook. Again, in 1803, he desired to return: again he was prevailed upon to stay. But the congratulations addressed to him by the Court on the brilliant successes of the earlier part of the Marátha war were coupled with a clause declaring that the Court did not enter 'at present into the origin or policy of the war.' This was felt by the imperious pro-consul as entirely invalidating the resolution of thanks.

'Never,' he wrote, 'have I been required to offer a greater or more painful sacrifice to public duty than that by which I renounced the satisfaction of publishing in India the marks of approbation and honour conferred upon me . . . but it appeared to me to be necessary to submit the high personal

[1] See Pellew's *Life of Lord Sidmouth*, vol. ii. pp. 77 sqq.

FINANCE, TRADE, AND THE DIRECTORS 161

distinction, which I should have derived from such a publication, to more important considerations of the public safety and of the interest of the Company and of the nation in India . . .

'The public and formal reservation of your judgement upon the justice of the war necessarily would have involved the possibility of your future condemnation of the cause in which the British arms had been employed. It could not be supposed that either your honourable Court or the Court of Proprietors would try the justice of our cause by the success of our arms ; the prosperous result of the war therefore could not have removed the doubts of its justice arising from the reservations expressed in your resolutions, and the irresistible inference in the minds of all the native states would have been, that your honourable Court and the Court of Proprietors might ultimately censure the whole transaction ; while the general fame of your equity and magnanimity would have precluded any supposition that in condemning the justice of our cause, you would retain the fruits of our success, or enjoy the benefits of the peace while you repudiated the necessity and policy of the war. The wisdom and prudence of your honourable Court will anticipate the confusion and disorder which must have arisen among the native powers if any doubt had been cast (without your express commands) by the public authority of this government upon the stability of a settlement of peace, concluded with the utmost degree of solemnity at the close of a most awful contest in arms, embracing the interests of every principal State in India, and establishing a comprehensive system of alliance and political relation over every region and province of Hindustán and the Deccan. If the origin and policy of the war shall ultimately be condemned, and the treaties of peace, partition, subsidy and alliance shall finally be abrogated by the commands of your honourable Court, those commands will be issued in such terms and accompanied by such arrangements as shall render the execution of your orders an additional bulwark to the public safety and a fresh security to the public faith. During whatever interval of time your honourable Court may be pleased to suspend your determination it would neither be consistent with the welfare of the honourable Company in India, nor with the respect due to your high authority, that one of your servants, forthe gratification of personal ambition by the ostentatious display of the honours which you had been pleased to confer upon him, should pursue a course which might embarrass the free and deliberate exercise of your wisdom and justice in a matter of the utmost importance to the national interests and honour; or that, by a premature and unseasonable publication of your favourable acceptance of his services, the same servant should risk the main object of those services, and endanger the immediate security of a great political system of arrangement which it may possibly be your future pleasure to confirm . . .

'I trust that your honourable Company and the Court of Proprietors will receive with favour the repeated expression of my sincere gratitude for the honour which you have been pleased to bestow upon me, and of my deep concern that the object of your liberal, generous, and public-spirited views, in conferring those high distinctions upon your principal servant in India, has been suspended by his conscientious sense of his duty to you, to the Company, and to the nation.'

The passage is so characteristic of the bitterest vein of Wellesley's irony, that so long a quotation may well be pardoned. It may be hoped that the Honourable Court were not insensible to the lash. We cannot wonder that the Governor-General should now write to Castlereagh of his 'utter contempt of any opinion entertained by the Court of Directors,' and of their 'vindictive profligacy':—

'Your Lordship,' he said, 'may be assured that as no symptom of tardy remorse displayed by the honourable Court in consequence of my recent successes will vary my present estimation of the faith and honour of my very worthy and approved good masters, or protract my continuance in India for one hour beyond the limits prescribed by the public interests, so no additional outrage, injury, or insult which can issue from the most loathsome den of the India House will accelerate my departure when the public safety shall appear to require my aid in this most arduous situation [1].'

But the Court by no means ceased from condemnation. Early in 1805 they repeated their censure of his disobedience, appointments, and expenditure, and the Board of Control added a remark on his repeated absence from the sessions of his Council.

Thus, while the Government rewarded Lake with a peerage, and Arthur Wellesley with the Order of the Bath, the Governor-General still remained suspended in mid air between admiration and displeasure.

He was eager to be gone, and when the news of Monson's disaster caused the immediate appointment of Cornwallis as his successor, it is probable that the Governor-General was the happiest man in India, that now at last he might leave it. It is said that he first obtained news of the reappointment of Cornwallis in conversation with Mr. Tucker: on May 25, he received Castlereagh's letter announcing it. On

---

[1] June 19, 1804; given in Pearce, *Life of Wellesley*, vol. ii, pp. 361, 2.

July 30, Cornwallis arrived at Calcutta, and took the oaths, and on August 15, Wellesley sailed for England. He knew that his policy would be reversed: but he knew too, we cannot doubt, that time would have his revenges and bring in again the principles on which he had founded and ruled the British Empire of India. There was sincerity and truth in the words with which the British inhabitants of Calcutta greeted him as he prepared to make his last formal and public appearance in their midst.

'The events of the last seven years,' said their address, 'have marked the period of your government as the most important epoch in the history of European power in India. Your discernment in seeing the exigencies of the country and of the times in which you were called to act, the promptitude and determination with which you have seized on the opportunities of acting, your just conception and masterly use of our intrinsic strength have eminently contributed in conjunction with the zeal, the discipline, and the courage of our armies to decide upon these great events; and to establish from one extremity of this empire to the other the ascendency of the British name and dominion [1].'

[1] *Wellesley Despatches*, vol. v. p. 613.

CHAPTER VIII

LATER LIFE

WELLESLEY returned to Europe with every hope of meeting with a reception worthy of his fame. His brother William [1] was successful and respected in the political world. His brother Arthur had been in England a year, and had reported how favourably disposed was the Ministry towards him. Pitt was still his staunch friend, and so warm was his personal feeling that when there was question of an attack in Parliament he actually consulted with Lord Grenville, from whom he was then utterly removed in politics, as to a defence in the Lords and Commons. On the other hand the Whigs were eager, it seemed, to secure so valuable an ally. 'Bucky,' wrote Arthur Wellesley after a visit ('a bore for two days') to Stowe, 'is very anxious that you should belong to the opposition.' But public opinion, then as now, was sluggish and ill informed in Indian matters. There was hesitation in England about the Marátha war, and misunderstanding about the Oudh treaty. It was clear that an attack would be made on the returned Governor-General. Arthur Wellesley advised

---

[1] Created Earl of Maryborough and afterwards succeeding to the Earldom of Mornington.

that it should be met by the Marquess himself in the Lords, and by Pitt, 'well charged with information,' in the Commons. Still on the whole the outlook was distinctly favourable, and Wellesley looked forward to something of a triumph on his return.

He was to learn how small a space his exploits filled in the minds of his countrymen. His reception at Portsmouth was cordial, polite; there were a few friends and some military and naval officials; but what a change from the solemn pageants which he had played in the East! Mr. Torrens tells—it is not clear on what authority—that his disgust and impatience could not be restrained. It is perhaps more probable that his self-command was superior to his indignation.

He had looked forward too, it may be, to a warm welcome in the domestic affections: here also it is clear that before long he was disappointed. Home life plays so small a part in all we know of Wellesley— he was so essentially stern and self-contained, so clearly public and not private in his life, that we almost forget that he was married. Early in life he had formed a connexion with a brilliant Frenchwoman whom he afterwards made his wife. Their children were not legitimate; but Society, then most lax in its views of the domestic relations, did not frown upon the mother or disparage the offspring. Lady Mornington had not accompanied her husband to India. The letters of his friends, particularly those of Lord Auckland, show that she was well cared for and beloved. But an union ill begun had not moral strength to carry it on, and the unhappily assorted pair separated soon after the Marquess's return. Lady Wellesley died in 1816. Her daughter married the first Lord Hatherton. Of their sons, Richard, the elder, won distinction as a politician, and held office at different times under Government; and Henry, the younger, was an Oxford tutor, Doctor of Divinity, and *virtuoso*. The latter showed considerable ability. He was an elegant writer and a refined man. He inherited his father's literary taste and had a valuable library, particularly rich in Italian books. As Principal of New Inn Hall he was well known and is still remembered at Oxford; and his excellent collection of engraved prints was in large part acquired by the University.

Wellesley was one of those men whose domestic life in no sense belongs to history. His first visit on his arrival was to his old friend Addington, now Lord Sidmouth; almost his first letter was to Pitt. The great statesman was, though he did not then know it, dying; and it was one of his last letters that reached the returning friend.

'My dear Wellesley,—On my arrival here (Putney) last night I received with inexpressible pleasure your most friendly and affectionate letter. If I was not strongly advised to keep out of London till I have acquired a little more strength I would have come up immediately, for the purpose of seeing you at the first possible moment. As it is, I am afraid I must trust to your goodness to give me the satisfaction of seeing you here the first hour you can spare for the purpose. If you can, without inconvenience, make it about the middle of the day (in English style, between two and four), it would suit me rather better than any other time; but none can be inconvenient. I am recovering rather slowly from stomach complaints followed by severe attacks of gout; but I believe I am now in the real way of amendment. Ever most truly and affectionately yours.— W. PITT[1].'

They met on January 13. Pitt was in high spirits, but Wellesley saw that the hand of death was upon him. It was a strange, sad meeting, between two great Englishmen, both, as it might seem, in the prime of life; one returned from the creation and the ruling of a great dominion, eager to lead and to command at home, the other with the reins of Empire slipping from his grasp: two loyal friends, whom the seas had severed, and who were reunited under the shadow of the dread summons to the testing and trial of a life's work. It was Wellesley who told friends and foes that death was at hand, and wrung from Grenville an agony of tears and an instant suspension of all criticism and opposition to the dying statesman; and Wellesley, it is clear, loved and admired him as he loved no other man.

Pitt's death deprived the returned Governor-General of a staunch defender. Instead of finding himself offered a post in the Government, he had to withstand attacks in the House of Commons. One Paull, a linendraper's son of Wisbeach, had been a trader at

---

[1] This letter is given both by Mr. Pearce, vol. ii. p. 386, and by Mr. Torrens, p. 202.

Lucknow when the purging of the Europeans was begun, and like other adventurers he had to discover that the hope of his gains was gone. Though he received some personal kindness from Wellesley he never forgave his action. He left India in 1804, and soon bought a seat in Parliament, where he endeavoured, with the encouragement of such worthy supporters as Cobbett and the Prince of Wales, to achieve a reputation by denouncing the Governor-General. On January 27, Paull moved for papers concerning Oudh; he secured Lord Folkestone's assistance, and continued for some time snapping at the heels of the returned Pro-consul; he even laid on the table an Article of charge of high crimes and misdemeanours. It has been asserted that Wellesley was offered office but declined it till these accusations had been disposed of, but there appears to be no evidence to warrant the assertion. It is true, however, be the cause what it may, that he took no part in politics till the charges had been finally defeated and a resolution approving his policy had been carried in the Commons.

The occasion of his return to public life marked the subject to which he intended to devote himself—foreign affairs. It was when the truculent conduct of the Government, in the seizure of the Danish fleet, was called in question in the House of Lords. Wellesley defended the action: it was a bold blow which would save much bloodshed. One check had been offered to Napoleon's unbroken successes. All Europe had been at his feet. The Delphic oracle, quoted Wellesley, spoke only in the Macedonian dialect. It was a memorable achievement, then, to mar one of his projects, and to stay, for however short a time, the progress of his chariot. The speech was in his old style, precise yet full of fire; and it was thought to be the ablest defence that the Ministry obtained. It was delivered on February 8, 1808, and it marked on the part of the speaker the foundation of an adhesion to the Ministry which was cemented by a growing sympathy with Canning.

Wellesley had now had time to scan both parties and men. It is clear that he preferred to keep aloof from the ordinary combinations, but was able to co-operate cordially with the Foreign Secretary. They had one view of the policy of opposition to Napoleon. They both believed in popular enthusiasm and sought to foster it. Wellesley, like his brother Arthur, condemned the ridiculous Walcheren expedition, and urged a decided intervention in the Spanish war. After Coruña, and Sir Arthur's temporary supersession, it was decided that an active policy in Spain was needed; and while the soldier was sent back to the Peninsula as General-in-Chief, the statesman was delegated Ambassador Extraordinary to his Catholic Majesty. When he heard that the chief force was to be sent on a fool's errand to Walcheren, the Marquess resigned his appointment, but he was induced to take it up again, and after some delay sailed for Spain, and landed at Cadiz on July 31, 1809.

His reception was a magnificent one. As he landed[1] he was received with every demonstration of public honour: when he entered Seville the whole city waited to welcome and applaud[2]. His task was to secure prompt and adequate support to his brother's army. The general had written that the troops were living on half allowance, and the cavalry could find forage only in the fields. Weary months were passed, during which the troops starved, and their commander chafed at inaction and delay; while the Ambassador wrote letter after letter, each more pressing than the last, to the junta and to the government at home. He submitted to the junta plans for the reconstruction of the government and of the military system; he urged, he implored, he commanded, but in vain. It was only too evident that no help could be looked for from the Spanish government itself. Sir Arthur

---

[1] Mr. Torrens gives a story that he was plumed in brilliant green out of compliment to the Spaniards. Through the kindness of D. Manuel Gomez Imar and D. Rafael Altamira I am able to state that there is no evidence for this and that it is most improbable. 'Seiguora,' says D. Manuel Gomez Imar, 'que en 1809 hubiera en Sevilla ni en España afición al color verde, áno ser que el biógrafo inglés al recordar el capítulo del Quijote "El Caballero del verde gabán" dedujera que era el predilecto de los hidalgos y hacendados, puesto que así vestía D. Diego de Miranda.' I owe the valuable assistance of these Spanish scholars to my friend Mr. H. Butler Clarke.

[2] A ludicrous incident is recorded by Mr. Torrens, which surely would not have escaped the notice of Mr. Jacob who was present (see reference to his book in Pearce, vol. iii. p. 23, viz. that the Maid of Saragossa, a strapping damsel, seized the haughty envoy and carried him up the grand staircase of the Town Hall, depositing him on the top with a resounding kiss.

Wellesley (who had been created Viscount Wellington) was compelled to retreat to Portugal.

It was clear to Canning that some bolder counsels at home were necessary to arouse and to support a national resistance to Napoleon. Castlereagh was not the man to carry out such a policy, and Canning sought to replace him as Foreign Secretary by the Marquess of Wellesley.

Then came the duel—a foolish precedent which the Duke of Wellington himself followed years later. The duel led to a reconstruction of the Ministry, and on December 6, Wellesley, summoned in hot haste from Spain, took the oaths and kissed hands as Foreign Secretary. His eldest son Richard was given a seat in Parliament, and a few weeks later he himself received the Garter. The investiture took place on March 10, 1810. Henry Wellesley, a few days after, was made Ambassador in his room; and it thus became patent that strenuous efforts would be made to support the Peninsular force.

But the Foreign Secretary had a hard task. Public feeling was strongly against the Spanish expedition: the Common Council of London, representative of many another public body, petitioned for its recall; and Wellesley, almost alone in England, prevented what would have been an European disaster. He spoke vigorously, he acted promptly, and eventually he was rewarded. On June 10, 1810, he said in the House of Lords:—

'With the fate of Spain the fate of England is inseparably

blended. Should we not therefore stand by her to the last? For my part, my lords, as an adviser to the Crown, I shall not cease to recommend to my Sovereign to continue to assist Spain to the latest moment of her existence. It should not dishearten us that Spain appears to be in the very crisis of her fate; we should, on the contrary, extend a more anxious care over her at a moment so critical. For in nations, and above all in Spain, how often have the apparent symptoms of dissolution been the presages of new life and of renovated vigour? Therefore I would cling to Spain in her last struggle; therefore I would watch her last agonies; I would wash and heal her wounds, I would receive her parting breath, I would catch and cherish the last vital spark of her expiring patriotism. Nor let this be deemed a mere office of pious charity, nor an exaggerated representation of my feelings, nor an overcharged picture of the circumstances that call them forth. In the cause of Spain the cause of honour and of interest is equally involved and inseparably allied; it is a cause in favour of which the finest feelings of the heart unite with the soundest dictates of the understanding.'

He had to fight many a hard battle in the Lords against some of his oldest friends; he had to keep up the enthusiasm of a Cabinet which it is easy to see was far from certain about the wisdom of the Spanish policy; he had to face the indignation of the people who were furious at the Spanish war and the imprisonment of Sir Francis Burdett. On the evening of April 6, the windows of Apsley House were broken: it was a scene to which the inmates were to become accustomed. Still Wellesley held steadfastly to his post, and his indomitable persistency carried his colleagues with him, till at length Wellington's urgent demands for money to feed his own and the

Portuguese troops were met as soon as they were made, and at the beginning of May 'money was sent in profusion to him; soldiers he wanted none.'

The Foreign Secretary had also to deal with the American difficulty, which sprang from the Berlin and Milan decrees and the Orders in Council; and he had to take part in drawing up the limitations under which the Prince of Wales was called upon to assume the Regency. The occasion of the first reading of the Regency Bill in the House of Lords has appeared to some to be a crisis in his life. He was expected, and prepared, to speak. No one was so competent; no one would have been listened to with such respect. But, in some extraordinary way, a nervousness overpowered him: he remained absolutely silent: and it was thought from that moment that his chances of the highest political power were gone. 'It augured,' wrote a gossip of the day, '*un homme passé*: and the most dangerous symptom of the whole was that he entirely agreed in the opinion.' To the astonishment of the well-informed, the Regent retained the Ministry in office, and Wellesley continued his efforts on behalf of the war. This was the whole *raison d'être* of his official position: on no other question of the day was he really cordial with his colleagues. He absented himself from many meetings of the Cabinet, and he voted against the Ministry when the question of Emancipation came up in the form of the Catholic petition on June 18, 1811.

[1] Torrens, *Wellesley*, p. 426.

At length it seemed that his efforts were being rewarded. Alexander I was drawing towards England. Europe began to awake to the service rendered by the Spanish resistance, and new life was springing up in Germany. Wellesley worked the harder the more the tide turned. The records of the Foreign Office show his untiring energy and enthusiastic zeal. 'It was his sanguine belief,' wrote the correspondent already referred to, 'that the face of Europe was about to undergo the most material change for the better, and all brought about by his counsels.' It is even certain that by unwearied patience and the use of all the arts, witty and brilliant, of which he was the master, he aroused in the idle voluptuary who exercised the functions of Royalty an interest and a zest in the European struggle. He was constantly with the Regent, and it seemed that he was destined to be Prime Minister before long. It appeared as if not even the Roman Catholic question—on which he actually sent in his resignation, though there proved to be no satisfactory means of filling his place— could unseat him. He made a speech in which he practically broke with the old Tories without being welcomed by the Whigs, but which marked his conscientious adherence to the liberal views that had always governed his action on the question.

There were weeks of shuffling. The Prince Regent was outwardly cordial, but in the background he was scheming for a change; and on February 19, 1812, Wellesley at last gave up the seals. He refused to be Lord Lieutenant of Ireland: he would not rest for a moment under the suspicion of agreement with the narrow views of the Prime Minister, Perceval. When, three months later, the Premier was shot, he received a request to return to office with Canning, but both declined to compromise their principles. Wellesley wrote to Lord Liverpool two letters, masterpieces of argument, which entirely vindicated his consistency. A few days later he had actually in his hands the making of a Ministry, but the chiefs of opposing factions would not coalesce. Catholic Emancipation and the vigorous prosecution of the war in Spain—on these two points Wellesley insisted, and on these bases it proved impossible to form a strong government[1]. There was no making peace between those who sought emancipation and those who hated it, and Wellesley declared in the House of Lords that 'the most dreadful personal animosities' made his task impossible.

The result of it all was the formation of Lord Liverpool's Ministry, which it was thought would last only a few months, but which lasted for fifteen years—the apotheosis of middle class commonplace. When the appointments became known there was an acrimonious discussion in the House of Lords, from which Wellesley came out easily victorious. But his chance of being Prime Minister was gone for ever.

On July 1, 1812, Wellesley made a motion in favour

---

[1] Wellesley published the *Correspondence and Documents explaining the proceedings in the recent negotiation for the formation of an Administration*, 1812.

of a consideration of the Roman Catholic claims: he delivered one of his best speeches, rhetorical in his familiar fashion, but with genuine conviction. He was defeated by one vote. Henceforth his exertions in the cause were silent, but he was none the less active.

The news of Salamanca, July 22, 1812, suddenly altered his position in the public eye. The splendid victory which showed decisively the greatness of Arthur Wellesley's military genius, and augured with no doubtful auspices the final triumph in Spain, brought both brothers at once to the top of the tide in popular favour. Wellington was made a Marquess. Wellesley felt that his judgement, so long contested and satirized, was at last justified. He joined enthusiastically in the jubilations of the London crowd. He shared himself in the triumph. Two years before his windows had been broken by the mob: now they drew his carriage to St. Paul's and the Mansion House, and brought him home with an ovation.

During the next few years Wellesley took but slight part in politics. One of his great objects was attained, the other for the time was unattainable. He signed—it is understood indeed that with Lord Grenville he composed—the admirable protest of eleven peers against the monstrous bill of the Government—a bill which to-day appears a work of almost incredible folly—by which all foreign corn was absolutely excluded from England till native wheat should fetch eighty shillings a quarter. Adam Smith was not forgotten: it was a measure, said the protest, by which a bounty was given to the grower of corn through a tax levied on the consumer.

Wellesley protested again and again as time went on against the Government's repressive policy in Ireland, and at home against the lavish armaments and the excessive taxation. He never feared to stand against class interests or public feeling. As he had urged the war when all were against it, so he opposed the resistance to Napoleon on his escape from Elba. In one of his speeches we hear the sound, unwonted indeed in those days of callous self-satisfaction, of the movement for social regeneration which has still to be accomplished :—

'When he saw the condition of all ranks of his Majesty's people and looked back to their exertions, their patience, their loyalty, their confidence in Parliament, and their present misery, he was utterly at a loss to conceive by what criminal forgetfulness of their duty ministers could have withheld the most solemn assurances of an immediate and strict enquiry into the causes of such tremendous misfortunes, and a pledge of every possible relief. The scandalous profusion could not go on: Parliament must do its duty: there was no longer a refuge to be found from the cry of the hungry, the famished population. The army must be reduced. . . . The Civil List also and all the establishments of every kind must be retrenched with no sparing hand. Indeed, one rule should be applied to them all, that nothing, however ancient, should be suffered to exist which was not absolutely necessary for the safety and very being of the country [1].'

Brave words from such a man! But he was no demagogue or mob leader; he would be as fearless in

[1] Given in Pearce's *Wellesley*, vol. iii. p. 312.

meeting the dangers of popular violence as in redressing the popular wrongs. He supported the Six Acts of 1819; he recognised the grim spectre of disaffection that stood behind the 'Manchester Massacre.'

At the end of 1821 Wellesley was offered and accepted the post of Lord Lieutenant of Ireland. The condition of the country was such as we have learnt to know only too well. Outrages were frequent, there was no control of the country districts, moonlighting and mob law prevailed. Wellesley was greeted as the harbinger of conciliation. His old friend Grenville had taken office: the Government looked less narrow: the House of Lords had begun to reject complete Emancipation by dwindling majorities. Wellesley and his brother were the two greatest living Irishmen; and thus the spectacle was seen, so rare afterwards on the entry of a Viceroy, of a magnificent reception by all parties alike. At his first Levée on January 8, 1822, he answered the Dublin address with well chosen words:—

'I have been called upon to serve my Sovereign and my country in various stations and in distant climates; wherever my lot has been cast I have endeavoured not to disgrace my family or my country. Now, if under the favour of my Gracious Sovereign and of Divine Providence, I should be enabled to restore peace and concord to Ireland, my long public career will be closed with happiness, honour, and genuine glory [1].'

In a banquet given a few days later he took opportunity to show how proudly he regarded the achieve-

[1] Pearce, iii. 321.

ments of his brother, and assured the company of the Duke's unalterable affection for his native country.

His earliest measures in Ireland were such reconstructions of the official patronage as should bring forward men more in sympathy with the wants of Ireland. Thus Mr. Plunket became Attorney-General and Mr. Burke Chief Justice. He began under the brightest auspices. Every one was willing to expect the best from him; even the irreconcilable eccentric, Sir Francis Burdett, complimented him on his sympathy with the people.

Wellesley's errand was certainly what is called nowadays a 'message of conciliation;' but, like many a Viceroy since his time, he found that he could not govern without 'coercion.' His earliest report to the home government showed how utterly unable was the ordinary law to cope with the disorder:—

'No additional military force,' he said, in a despatch submitted to Parliament at the beginning of the Session, in February, 1822, 'no improvement nor augmentation of the police would now be effectual without the aid of the Insurrection Act; with that aid it appears to me to be rational to expect that tranquillity may be maintained, confirmed, and extended throughout Ireland.'

The Act was passed, and the Habeas Corpus Act was suspended. Ribbonmen were brought to trial, and traitorous associations were broken up. Wellesley's letters and those of the Irish law officers show that his policy was to substitute a fear of the majesty of the Law for the terrorism of conspirators and secret societies. Within a year (January 29, 1823) he was able to report a great diminution of crime, and to advocate with the conviction of experience the renewal of the Insurrection Act for another year, and the reform of the Irish magistracy and police. Where he could himself act in this direction he acted with vigour. He struck off the Commission of the Peace several hundreds of magistrates who were known to be party men. He actively inaugurated Relief Funds for the starving peasantry, subscribed a large sum himself, and got together a handsome amount.

But we seem to be recording events with which we are only too familiar. Fiendish crime and childish folly were then as now the staples of Irish agitation. The palpable parallels of Irish history confront us at every step. Philanthropy and conciliation were alike fruitless: repression was effectual only over a limited area.

On July 12, 1822 [1], the Orange demonstration round the Statue of King William on College Green was prevented; but when the Irish determine on a 'bit of fun' there is no separating without broken heads, and Dublin was for days a scene of disorder. Roman Catholics and Irish Churchmen fought each other and the King's troops, and the Lord Mayor could only

---

[1] For these occurrences see *One Year of the Administration of his Excellency the Marquess of Wellesley in Ireland*, 1823, a bitter and ironical attack; *Recent Scenes and Occurrences in Ireland*, 1823, a reply to the former; *Reflections on the Lieutenancy of the Marquess Wellesley*, 1824, a strong eulogium on the conciliatory policy and its success.

quell the riot by a strong military force. The disturbances were renewed on November 5, and the excitement lasted over a month. On December 14, with all the Irish zest in a 'row,' the Lord Lieutenant attended the Theatre Royal in State with a large suite. The occasion was not to be missed. The brave Protestant boys saw their opportunity. Placards were distributed with the watchwords of 'No Popery,' 'The Protestants want Talbot as the Papists have got all but!!!' and 'Ex-Governor of the Bantams shall change his Morning-tone.' Wellesley must have known well that there would be a scene; but probably he did not expect a quart bottle at his head. This, however, was what he received when he stood up at 'God save the King.' Fortunately the aim was not equal to the intention, and the little Viceroy suffered nothing worse than the cat-calls and groans which greeted his entrance and exit. Unfortunately he did not take this display of Irish humour in a humorous spirit. Several of the rioters were prosecuted for treasonable conspiracy; the Grand Jury threw out the bill, and a vote of Censure on the prosecution was moved in the House of Commons which it needed all Plunket's great oratory to rebut.

Meanwhile the control of Lord Liverpool's administration had, by the suicide of Castlereagh on August 12, 1822, passed into the hands of Canning, and Wellesley, more secure of support in his policy of conciliation, was applying himself to the production of a scheme to settle the tithe question. An interesting letter printed by Mr. Pearce shows Lord Dacre exchanging views with the Viceroy and preparing a plan to regulate the tithe by a septennial average, such as was afterwards adopted for England.

These efforts were characteristic of Wellesley's viceroyalty. He was not a popular ruler: he had none of the arts of the demagogue: he was a genuine philanthropist and a far-sighted statesman. His work was not showy, but it was pre-eminently the work that Ireland needed, and through him the Irish administration received an impress which it ought never to have lost. The contrast that was presented by his successors was wittily expressed by Wellesley himself. Lord Normanby, who replaced him after his second tenure of office in 1834, went round Ireland opening the prisons to every sort of criminal, with that idle disregard of honour which has developed into a tenderness for 'mere murder.' 'Ah,' said Wellesley, comparing his successor to the king in *Tom Thumb*, 'he has made mercy blind instead of justice.'

Wellesley's viceroyalty lasted throughout the administration of Canning and Lord Goderich—so long, that is, as Roman Catholic Emancipation remained an open question in the Cabinet. He resigned in January, 1828, when his brother became Prime Minister on the lines of distinct Protestant ascendancy. His resignation was the signal for the beginning of a serious and determined agitation in Ireland. It was followed almost immediately by the Clare Election.

'The time is come,' said Daniel O'Connell, 'when the system pursued towards this country must be put a stop to. It will not do for the future to say "Sweet friend, I wish you well," but it must be shown by acts that they do wish us well. It is time that this system should be put an end to; and I am come here to put an end to it.' Wellesley's aim was at last to be accomplished.

The resignation of the Marquess was an evident sign of his divergence from the Duke. A breach between the brothers had long been forming, and now the divergence was complete. 'The duke,' as Mr. Thursfield well says [1], 'could never understand that the old toryism was dead.' The Marquess had never been an old Tory. It is clear enough from the sayings which gentlemen of his household remember— at least one distinguished member of his Court (the Hon. Charles Gore) is still living, and recalls some pointed expressions to that effect—that he held a very poor opinion of his brother's political ability. It is clear, too, that he could not help feeling that while he had given to his brother in India the opportunities which he so well used to lay the foundation of his greatness, the Duke had in later years done little or nothing to repay the obligation.

On June 10, 1828, they opposed each other in the House of Lords. Wellesley wisely and temperately urged the abandonment of the antiquated injustice: Roman Catholic exclusion was no longer a security;

---

[1] *Peel (Twelve English Statesmen)*, p. 93.

it had become a positive and pressing danger. 'He supported the claims of the Roman Catholics from solemn conviction, founded on long and studious attention to the operation in Ireland of the laws enacted for their exclusion.' Wellington replied that he regarded the disabilities as indispensable securities for the safety of Church and State. Before a year was over the Duke himself carried what he was then opposing. On the Reform question the circumstances were repeated. Wellesley had for years been an ardent reformer: Wellington held out till concession was considered more pusillanimous than public-spirited. Well did Wellesley say to Lord Combermere, 'Arthur is a great soldier, but he will never make a statesman.' He used stronger words to another of his friends.

Differences on political questions were not the only causes of disagreement. It had been expected that the elder brother would obtain high office on a change of Ministry. Lord Goderich had recommended his addition to the Cabinet. It was thought that when Wellington was asked to form a Government he would place his brother at the head of it. But the famous caricature of Leech was already prefigured[1]: 'the Greedy Boy' would not let any one who might be deemed a rival 'have any of the nice things.'

When Lord Grey's Government came in Wellesley

---

[1] Leech's Cartoon in *Punch* on the Debate in the House of Lords, June 5, 1846, when Wellington voted against conferring distinctions on Hardinge and Gough.

was made Lord Steward of the Household, and after the passing of the Reform Bill became again Lord Lieutenant of Ireland. His son-in-law, Mr. Littleton, was now Chief Secretary for Ireland, and they together drew up proposals which, if carried, might have been a real relief to the disappointed feelings of the Irish patriots. A Coercion Act was in force, and its most stringent clauses were renewed contrary to the advice of both Wellesley and Littleton. Their suggestions included the admission of Roman Catholics to the Judicial Bench, to the Privy Council, and to other civil offices, high and low: and it was Wellesley's wise motion on the Irish tithe question which caused the defeat of Peel's Ministry.

In Lord Grey's second administration Wellesley was for a few weeks Lord Chamberlain, and no public explanation was ever given of his retirement. He was now seventy-five, and it was not surprising that he gave up public life altogether [1]. His last appearances were marked by compliments from the leaders of both political parties: Peel, Grey, and Melbourne united to honour him.

The next seven years were spent in seclusion.

'For years past,' wrote Greville in 1833, 'he has lived entirely out of the world. He comes to the House of Lords,

---

[1] Cf. *Greville Memoirs*, iii. 103, 110. The explanation he gave in the House of Lords was considered to explain nothing. Mr. Gore writes to me, 'It was not unnatural that with his great ability and the fame to which he had attained, he should upon reflection have felt the appointment of Lord Chamberlain as a degradation.' But there was probably more in it.

talks of making a speech every now and then, of which he is never delivered, and he comes to Court, where he sits in a corner and talks (as those who know him say) with as much fire and liveliness as ever, and with the same neat, shrewd causticity that formerly distinguished him [1].'

Witty himself, wit flourished in his society. A distinguished member of his Viceregal Household recalls an amusing example. The late Lord Albemarle (then Captain Keppel), his Aide-de-Camp, had returned overland from India to Europe and wrote a 'Personal Narrative' of his travels. At dinner one day, just after the publication of the book, Lord Wellesley asked Lord Plunket, who was one of the guests—' Plunket, what do you understand by a Personal Narrative '— ' My Lord,' replied the Chancellor, ' in Law we call all personal that is not real.'

Wellesley's first wife had died in 1816. In October 1825 he married Mrs. Patterson, a beautiful and accomplished American, sister to the Duchess of Leeds and Lady Stafford. They lived happily. In a copy of his *Primitiae et Reliquiae* (published in 1840) which he gave to her he wrote these lines of Dryden :—

> ' All of a tenour was their after life,
> No day discoloured with domestic strife,
> No jealousy but mutual truth believed,
> Secure repose and kindness undeceived.'

During these last years, spent chiefly at Kingston House, Brompton, Wellesley's chief friend was Lord

[1] *Greville Memoirs*, iii. 31.

Brougham, to whom he was sincerely attached. Greek epigrams passed between them week by week. Brougham in 1838 dedicated his speeches to his venerable friend 'as a tribute most justly due to so illustrious a statesman, and in commemoration of the rare felicity of England, so rich in genius and capacity for affairs that she can spare from her service such men as he.'

Wellesley had never ceased to cultivate literature and scholarship. In the last year of his life he published poems, Latin and English, written at different dates, with the characteristic motto :—

> 'Valido mihi
> Latos dones, et, precor, integra
> Cum mente, nec turpem senectam
> Degere, nec cithara carentem.'

Many of these *Primitiae et Reliquiae* have that curious felicity of expression for which he was renowned, and there are frequent traces of genuine feeling. Greville's story of his rehearsing speeches which he never delivered has been quoted. It had been observed, many years before, by Pitt, that he was extraordinarily slow in composition as well as elaborate in preparation, but there would be no reason for his timidity at this date. He would have received an ovation if he had entered the House. But he had abandoned politics, and had put his proxy at the service of Peel.

In September, 1835, Mr. Montgomery Martin applied to the Marquess to allow the publication of his

Indian Despatches. They were brought out in the following year, with a dedication to the King.

'It becomes not the Editor,' says the preface to the fourth volume, 'to express here his feelings for the confidence reposed in him by the nobleman whose wise, humane, and patriotic government it has been his anxious wish to place in a full and clear light before the public. To have contributed in any manner, however humbly, towards the accomplishment of such a truly national object will ever be to him a source of grateful remembrance and happiness.'

It was now time for the Directors of the East India Company to make the *amende honorable*. A wiser spirit had come over the counsels of Leadenhall Street, and it was recognised that to Wellesley England owed the creation of an Empire. The Directors ordered a number of copies of the book to be distributed in India, and, in a complimentary correspondence that ensued they assured the Marquess that they were convinced that the Despatches 'were made public in the same spirit in which they were composed—an ardent zeal to promote the well being of India and to uphold the interest and honour of the British Empire.'

They did not stop at compliment. Hearing that the Marquess was not well off the Court voted him the sum of £20,000; and in March 1841 they decided to place a marble statue of him in the India House as 'a public, conspicuous, and permanent mark of the admiration and gratitude of the East India Company.' All his old dignity and rhetorical feeling was seen in his reply to the Directors' letter.

'My first emotion,' he says, 'was to offer up my thankful acknowledgements to the Almighty power which has preserved my life beyond the ordinary limits of human nature, to receive a distinction of which history affords so few, if any, examples. ... May the memorial by which you are pleased to distinguish my services remind you of the source from which they proceed and of the ends to which they were directed; and confirm the principles of public virtue, the maxims of public order, and a due respect for just and honest government.'

He was not to die without a reconciliation with his brother. In May 1838, the Duke of Wellington came to see him, and their differences were forgotten. The affection of the elder brother for the younger had been tested in a hundred ways: he had strenuously defended him throughout his early career, and given him the opportunities without which his powers might never have been displayed; and Wellington, with all his divergence from his brother's views, yet bore testimony to his greatness: in all the distinctions of his life, he said, he had never forgotten the honour of being Lord Wellesley's brother.

Wellesley died on September 26, 1842, at the age of eighty-two. By his own wish he was buried at Eton, to which ancient foundation he had been so long a devoted son. In the midst of his Indian triumphs his heart had turned fondly towards his two boys there at school, and in his *Primitiae et Reliquiae* he had again and again paid tribute to the noble College. His two surviving brothers, the able diplomatist and the great soldier, whose abilities he had fostered and on whose behalf he had undergone so much unmerited obloquy, followed his body to the grave. We may find his best epitaph in the words which Sir William Fraser[1] attributes to the Iron Duke, 'There is a great man gone.'

[1] It is painful to insinuate a doubt where the saying is so characteristic and the incident so well told. Sir W. Fraser, *Words on Wellington*, 1889, says that the Duke received the news by letter at Walmer: but Lord Stanhope, *Notes of Conversation with the Duke of Wellington*, who was staying at Walmer at the time, says the Duke brought the news from London himself.

CHAPTER IX

THE GREAT PROCONSUL: HIS FAME AND ACHIEVEMENTS

To the illustrious statesman whose biography he sketched so felicitously, Mr. Torrens gave the title of 'the great Proconsul.' The phrase was an apt one. In the area over which he exercised his delegated powers, in the principles on which he ruled, in his personal character, just, despotic, cultured, Richard Wellesley recalled one of those great governors through whose mighty deeds old Rome left so deep an impress on the nations of East and West. Compared to many of his contemporaries, statesmen of renown, he seems to stand upon another plane; he is not of their world. The petty details of intrigue, the narrow ken of Whig and Tory policy, he is outside all these. What is it to him who is made judge or bishop, it is his to work for great issues and for great issues only. However we may estimate his success as a statesman it is impossible to deny the loftiness or the purity of his aims. Wellesley, though in his own time many of his inferiors distanced him in the race for public position, will ever rank among the greatest men of the century, and the marks that he has left upon the history of his nation will remain while time shall last.

We cannot judge the character, we can but imperfectly estimate the worth, till we know of the hero what manner of man he was. 'His person,' says his earliest biographer, Mr. Pearce, 'was small and symmetrical—his face remarkable for intellectual beauty —and his whole deportment elegant and dignified. He possessed a fine manly voice, and delivered his sentiments in public with great perspicuity and effect.' This is a brief and not very expressive description which the aid of portraits and statues, as well as the memory of many men still living, enables us to eke out.

His was a face which painters were eager to depict. Hoppner, ever sympathetic, painted him before he went out to India, and the portrait, which was exquisitely engraved in mezzotint by Young, is a singularly beautiful work. The complexion is clear and youthful. The keen deep-set eyes look out from under a mass of half-tumbled hair. The mouth is firm but slightly pouting, with a curious contraction of the upper lip. The expression is strangely attractive and winning, as of one who felt deeply and loved much, a poet, a musician, a great writer. But in the alertness of the gaze, the arched nostril, the long straight nose, there are the signs of an eager spirit, bold, commanding, originative. It is a face no one could look on without admiration or without respect. The mien is of one who expected obedience, but who could trust and be trusted.

Later on, Robert Home, a Scotsman who went out to Calcutta and painted many a blond civilian and swarthy Nawáb, drew the Governor-General in his state dress with the star of St. Patrick on his breast. This picture was engraved by Heath in 1804. In 1827 Robertson painted him in his Garter robes— a full-length showy picture of a handsome man of middle age, the hair thin and whitening—dignified, stately, attuned to pomp and pageantry. Most widely known of all the portraits, through the many engravings of it which were produced, is that by Sir Thomas Lawrence. But it has hardly the sympathy which touches the best work of that gentle master. Here the Marquess is taken with almost full face, in morning dress, the George hanging on his breast. The eye and the eyebrows are characteristic, but the whole picture is rather handsome than expressive. This smooth face, we feel, may be a poet's or that of the head of some ancient house; it does not proclaim the ruler of men. Another portrait said to be by the same master hangs in the hall of Christ Church, Oxford. There the Marquess is drawn full length, in Garter robes—but the picture is barren and uninspiring. There are two beautiful miniatures in the library at Eton. Count d'Orsay, whom Wellesley in the lighter aspects of his character not a little resembled, drew a bold sketch of him in the last year of his life. Here he looks old, but hardly the eighty-two years which he wore, as it seems, so lightly. The hair that is still left is snow-white now, but the thick bushy eyebrows are black as jet. In the falling in of the mouth the strong powerful chin comes out more than ever, and the nose grows more like the Iron Duke's. Still a smile plays about the thin lips and the gaze is keen, unfaltering, but touched with pathos. Truly, in the last year of his life, his eye was not dimmed nor his natural force abated.

At Calcutta the British residents erected a marble statue of him, which was placed in the hall of the Government House which he had erected. The other statues, and the bust by Nollekens, lack the beauty of the best pictures; but in all, the keen deep-set eye and the arched and bushy brows appear.

There is little trace in any of the portraits of the delicacy which all Wellesley's contemporaries note. When he was young his health was far from strong, and he was obliged to take great care of himself. His health at eighty-two, vigorous and hale, was the more surprising—so his nephew Gerald told Lord Stanhope a few months before his death—because at half that age it had seemed completely broken. When he went out to India, his brother Henry said, he was both ill and nervous, and he had quite determined to return home from the Cape, but was dissuaded. From his arrival in the East he seemed to win new vigour. 'My health,' he wrote to Lord Auckland in 1799, ' is and has uniformly been much better than it usually was in England; and the pressure and variety of business has been useful to my spirits.' Still there are many allusions in his correspondence to occasional attacks of illness, which beset him in times of anxiety but never prevented his mind from controlling the business and triumphing over the difficulties of his task. His constitution in fact was, like that of many another great man, not robust enough to be trifled with or to lure towards feats of rash experiment or endurance, but capable of meeting a great strain, strong in reserved force, the servant and not the master of a restless and buoyant will. 'It is difficult,' he once said of his work, 'but in these days difficulties are our daily food, and, for one, I find that I thrive upon it.'

What Wellesley lacked in physical strength he made up in *esprit*. He was well served by a bright sense of humour and a keen and natural Irish wit. He shone in society. In the brilliant circle which met at Holwood and Putney Hill, at Walmer and Wimbledon, he was one of the most brilliant members: in later days, we are told, half the beauties of London were at his feet. As a talker he could hold his own with the best: there is a tradition that Madame de Stael, when they met at Lansdowne House, had to own his superiority. As a wit his *bons mots* were constantly repeated, and used, by his friends.

He was a devoted lover of literature. His own style was modelled, somewhat too closely, on the classics. He admitted, says Lord Brougham, the vast superiority of Demosthenes, but he could not shake off his attachment to Cicero. He was renowned, indeed, among the pedants as a scholar: he could beat the schoolmasters at their own weapons; and, to do them justice, they paid him the homage of which they are not too lavish even to titled poets. He was as well read in the great moderns as in the classics. Again and again in his letters, and even in his despatches, a phrase of Shakespeare's, neatly and appropriately used, catches and delights the attentive ear. The Auction List of his Library shows his extensive acquaintance with the Italian poets. Dante he knew as few men of his age knew him. Lord Stanhope writes of a dinner party at Walmer in 1839—when the great statesman was in his eightieth year [1]—

'Lady Burghersh told me that lately calling on Lord Wellesley she had seen upon his table a print of Sir Joshua Reynolds's *Ugolino*, and, the conversation turning upon this, Lord Wellesley repeated several lines of Dante's description. She expressed her surprise at his power of memory, when he answered that he really thought, if he tried, he could repeat nearly the whole of that canto, and on trying he really did repeat above fifty lines of it. She was struck too, she said, with his pure and classic pronunciation of the Italian, and of that there could not be a more competent judge. I observed to her, that what enhanced the merits of these accomplishments was that they never could have proceeded from business or ambitious objects, as he never had any Italian mission to fulfil or Italian negotiations to conduct, so that love of literature must have been his only motive.'

[1] *Conversations with the Duke of Wellington*, pp. 169-170.

Lord Stratford de Redcliffe[1] told how in his last days of retirement he went to see him, and walked about with him in his garden and talked of politics. In the whole course of the conversation, he said, 'at one time figured the commanding statesman, at another the accomplished orator, to say nothing of wit, scholarship, and the recollection of bygone events.' Sir Walter Scott, a severe critic of conversational powers, wrote of him in 1825: 'The Marquess's talk gave me the notion of that kind of statesmanship that one might have expected from a Roman Emperor accustomed to keep the whole world in his view, and to divide his hours between ministers like Maecenas and wits like Horace.'

His schemes for the improvement of the education of Indian civilians are proofs of the liberality of his own studies. While the foundation was to be laid in a knowledge of the ancient classics of the West, the superstructure was to be built of different material. Like his great predecessor Warren Hastings, he recognised, as too few Englishmen did, the beauties, and the unique position, of the great Oriental literatures. He personally encouraged and patronized the learned men of Bengal, and under his auspices the talents of his own countrymen were directed towards the scholarship of the East.

[1] For this and several of these anecdotes I am indebted to an exceedingly interesting article in the *Quarterly Review*, vol. 169, No. 298.

In his personal character Wellesley could not be accused of the faults into which meaner natures fall. He was proud undeniably, but with the pride of a great, not a small, mind. 'No two brothers,' said Macaulay once, when Wellington and Wellesley were compared, 'were ever so unlike.' Rogers, describing them, said that they gave the most remarkable contrast in history, 'the one scorning all display, the other living for nothing else.' It was a sharp saying, such as the irresponsible conversationalist would readily throw off; and it has a certain superficial justice about it. But Wellesley loved display not for itself but as the outward sign of the dignity with which he was invested. His dressings and his attitudes, his ceremonies, attendances, and processions, his pageantry and extravagances, were part of his conception of the character of a British ruler in the East, or of a Viceroy among a Celtic people. He was tied to a constant series of ceremonial acts: it was clear to him that they lost all their value if they were not performed ceremoniously. Here was the contrast of his nature to the Englishmen among whom he moved, and who mocked, like Sheridan, at his airs and graces. The English love state and pomp as much as any other nation, but they like to see it done in hugger-mugger, with no dignity or order. An English procession is of all sights on the earth one of the most mirth-provoking. But a pageant *en déshabille* was to Wellesley a revolting anomaly. He delighted to impress, and he knew how to be impressive. To him dignity and a seemly order were the due appointments of life. He clung to the ceremonious features of the age before the Revolution. 'His indignation may be imagined,' says the writer of an interesting article in the *Quarterly Review*, 'when, as he was explaining some measure to the Cabinet, Lord Westmoreland leant back in his chair, in true American fashion, with his dirty boots resting on the Council table. Lord Wellesley paused and said: " When the Lord Privy Seal is in a decent attitude, I will proceed with my statement." '

Wellesley, immersed in ceremony, was the very type, said Sir James Mackintosh, of the 'sultanized Englishman.' His entertainments at Calcutta and Barrackpur are recorded in many an old Indian newspaper. The festivities at Government House to celebrate the Peace of Amiens are deemed worthy of a lengthy description by Mr. Pearce; and Lord Valentia, who visited Wellesley in India, describes his country retreat in glowing terms.

'The situation of this house,' he says, 'is much more pleasing than anything I have yet seen. It is considerably elevated above the Húglí river, on a very extended reach of which it stands: on the sides are pagodas, villages, and groves of lofty trees. The water itself is much clearer than at Calcutta, and covered with the state barges and cutters of the Governor-General. These, painted green and ornamented with gold, contrasted with the scarlet dresses of the rowers, were a great addition to the scene. The park is laid out in the English style, and the house is well adapted to the climate, having a beautiful verandah on every side, and the rooms being on a very ample scale [1].'

His Excellency, wearing the orders of St. Patrick and the Crescent in diamonds, was a prominent figure in the Calcutta balls. In the gay scene, writes the same witness of one of these festivities, 'the black dress of the male Armenians was pleasing from the variety; and the costly, though unbecoming habits of their females, together with the appearance of officers, nabobs, Persians and natives, resembled a masquerade [2].'

Of a piece with his magnificence in entertainment was the attitude which Wellesley assumed towards public works, the arts, and learning. He was not only himself a *virtuoso*; he was a patron in right of his position. Thus we find him, like the great rulers of the Renaissance, busy in schemes for the building and improvement of cities. A minute of June 16, 1803 [3], describes his plans for the improvement of Calcutta. He pointed out the deficiencies of the drainage and of the sanitary arrangements of all kinds. 'It is the primary duty,' he observed, ' of the Government to provide for the health, safety, and convenience of the inhabitants of this great town by

---

[1] *Voyages and Travels*, by George, Viscount Valentia, 1811 (dedicated to Lord Wellesley), vol. i. pp. 39, 40.　　[2] Ibid. vol. i. p. 37.

[3] *Wellesley Despatches*, vol. iv. pp. 672 sqq.

establishing a comprehensive system for the improvement of the roads, streets, public drains, and water courses; and by fixing permanent rules for the construction and distribution of the houses and public edifices, and for the regulation of nuisances of every description. The appearance and beauty of the town are inseparably connected with the health, safety, and convenience of the inhabitants, and every improvement which will introduce a greater degree of order, symmetry, and magnificence in the streets, roads, ghâts, and wharfs, public edifices and private habitations, will tend to ameliorate the climate and to secure and promote every object of a just and salutary system of police.'

We find him discussing in another minute[1] (July 26, 1804) the natural history of India. He appointed Dr. Francis Buchanan 'to collect materials for a correct account of all the most remarkable quadrupeds and birds in the provinces,' and invited information from all the medical officers in India. He established a 'Zoological Garden' at Barrackpur for the assistance of Buchanan's investigation. 'The illustration and improvement of that important branch of the natural history of India which embraces an object so extensive as the description of the principal parts of the animal kingdom is worthy of the munificence and liberality of the English East India Company, and must necessarily prove an acceptable service to the world. To facilitate and promote all enquiries which

[1] *Wellesley Despatches*, vol. iv. p. 674 sqq.

may be calculated to enlarge the boundaries of general science is a duty imposed on the British Government in India by its present exalted situation.' A year later he issued a valuable minute on the 'Improvement of Agriculture[1].' 'Independently of the moral duty imposed on the British Government to provide by every means in its power for the improvement of the condition of its subjects, substantial advantages must necessarily be derived by the State from the increased wealth and prosperity of the people.' He proposed to establish an experimental farm at Barrackpur, in which the improvement of the breed of black cattle, the introduction of a more scientific system of agriculture, and the reduction of the expense of preparing the grain for consumption, should be studied.

These are merely specimens of the range of his purview. It was his aim, indeed, to take place in all public affairs as the natural head and universal patron. The position was congenial to his mind: and it was reflected in his literary style. He was essentially a man of great ideas; and he clothed his thoughts in befitting language. Wellesley—Mr. Robert Louis Stevenson has said it with felicity of the British admirals—was not only great-hearted, he was big-spoken. A lofty strain, like the sound of martial and ceremonial music, breathes through his speeches; but his language expresses—it does not disguise—the greatness of his heart. The curious story that was

[1] June 1, 1803; *Wellesley Despatches*, iv. 676 sqq.

told of Wolfe, describing to the disgusted Pitt, in terms too glowing, and with action too expressive, the victories he would win in Canada, serves to show how a great man may for the moment borrow the cloak of the braggart. From such a scene Wellesley's good taste would have preserved him, but he would not have been without a certain sympathy for the chief actor. In something akin to this feature of his character we may find the clue to his failure to reach the supreme and highest greatness. While we recognise his achievements, we do not dream of comparing him to the still, strong heroes whom England has given to the East. We do not rank him with Dalhousie, with Havelock, with Gordon, or with that great man to whom tardy justice is at length being done, Warren Hastings, the greatest of them all.

Great, noble, in many ways, was Richard Wellesley, and his Indian career was undeniably magnificent, but we feel that there is something lacking throughout his life. Is it a moral quality we seek? The clue to it may lie in some aspect of his character of which national history is wont to take slight count. He was, say his contemporaries, what is called 'a man of pleasure;' and there is in such a character, however it may be, like his, gradually refined and purified, a taint which spreads subtly but surely to the public work. Self-seeking can never be wholly absent from the life where now and again pleasure holds the reins. Here is the flaw which mars what is, in many aspects, a beautiful soul. Mornington, refusing to share in the reward of the brave men who had shed their blood in the Mysore war, and Wellesley, walking in his Brompton garden, telling old tales with the genial charm of gracious and kindly age, are happier pictures than that of the companion of the 'Dandies,' and the man of whom Wilberforce wrote, 'I hear even worldly people take offence at his character for the head of the administration of the country.' A 'Sultanized Englishman,' in any of the meanings of that happy phrase, was not one to rule Great Britain.

Thus much must be said lest we seem to take too high a view of Wellesley's character and capacities, and to leave inexplicable the comparative failure of his life. Many worse men have played a greater part in English politics, and have left names more famous among English statesmen. But Wellesley scorned disguise: such as he was, with his defects and his honours, he stood forth. Proudly and not without disdain he met the judgement of his peers. He could not stoop, though it were for Empire. Like Coriolanus, he would say,

'I had rather be their servant in my way
Than sway with them in theirs.'

We may not wonder, then, that justice has not yet been done to his great qualities. When his papers are fully examined, and an exhaustive biography is written, he will appear, we may be confident, greater than the world now knows.

Meantime his achievements place him high in the ranks of our great worthies. He saw and tried to solve the eternal Irish question. He was a Freetrader before the days of the Manchester School. But for him, it may be truly said, it is more than probable that Napoleon would not have been overthrown. It was the Spanish resistance, as the Emperor himself recognised, that really destroyed him: and but for Wellesley's persistency, that resistance would never have been organized and brought to success. To his brother's indomitable and clear-sighted but unostentatious determination, Wellington owed the sinews of war, without which he could not possibly have coped with the French forces. It was Wellesley as well as Wellington who triumphed in the Peninsula.

But it is to his Indian administration incontestably that we look for the proofs of his greatness. As he gazed upon the great Eastern panorama, and then turned to his masters in Leadenhall Street, he may well have thought, 'I know that in this vast land I can create a British Empire, and I know that no other man can.' In India his work remains uneffaced and uneffaceable. He turned the East India Company, in spite of itself, from a trading corporation into an imperial power. He found the edifice of their rule fashioned of brick: he left it marble. Before his day the exigencies of the moment had guided British governors in a policy which even in the hands of its greatest exponents was empirical. Wellesley laid down lines from which it was impossible for his successors ever wholly to diverge. The experiment indeed was tried: Cornwallis set about to reverse all that he had done, and declared in so many words that his policy was mistaken and unsound. Barlow followed on the same tack; but Wellesley's system triumphed in the end.

He found India the battle-ground of races and of rulers. Every man's hand was against his neighbour. In the atrophy of government and the absence of any central controlling power, society was verging towards the state of nature as Hobbes pictured it. The life of man was, if rarely 'solitary,' often 'nasty, brutish, and short.' Wellesley taught the races where to look for union and for rule. He taught England how to estimate, and to enter upon, her heritage. Vast indeed was the dominion over which he caused the British flag to wave. He destroyed the cruel and threatening Muhammedan power in the South. He changed Oudh from a danger into a safeguard, and set Bengal free on every side from fear of foreign attack. He paralyzed if he did not destroy the hydra-headed confederacy of the Maráthás. He made the name of England honoured from Persia to the Red Sea: and he raised her fame in a way more durable than by military exploits. He taught her rulers, her civilians, her judges, to trust for their power only to the uprightness of their lives, the completeness of their labours, their knowledge of the character and the learning of the people committed to their charge. But he did more than this. It was the sign of his greatness and the mark of the permanence of his work that he recognised to the full the responsibility cast upon Great Britain. In his attitude towards commerce, diplomacy, war, religion, the same principle was patent and outspoken. In our hands, he would say, are the destinies of this mighty empire—to us belongs its development and its future: it is for England to raise it among the families of the nations —or we shall bear the blame for ever.

INDEX

ADDINGTON, Henry, Viscount Sidmouth, 25, 140, 159, 167.
AHMADNAGAR, taken, 94: ceded, 98.
ALÍGARH, capture of, 97.
ALÍ HUSAIN, 60.
AMERICANS, their commerce in India, 152.
ARGÁON, battle of, 96.
ASSAYE, battle of, 94–96.
AUCKLAND, Lord, friend of Wellesley's, 64, 167, 195.
AURANGÁBÁD, 94.
AZÍM U'D DAULAH, Nawáb of Karnátik, 60, 76.

BAIRD, Sir David, 21, 22, 44, 45, 130.
BARLOW, Sir John, opinion of treaty of Bassein, 90.
BASSEIN, treaty of, 86 *sqq.*
BENGAL, 94: bank of, 148 *note*: Presidency of, 113, 135–6.
BHARTPUR, Rájá of, 107: siege of, 107.
BHONSLA, 83, 86, 92, 94–96.
BOMBAY, Civil Service at, 29–30: address from, 52: proposal concerning, 113 *sqq.*
BOURQUIN, M. Louis, 97, 128.
BRAGG, Mr., opinion on the Indian government proposals of Wellesley, 115.
BROUGHAM, Lord, Wellesley's chief friend in his last years, 187–8.

BURDETT, Sir Francis, 173, 180.

CALCUTTA, address from, to Wellesley, 52: treaty at, in 1799, 62: Wellesley's reply to address from, 99: college at, 121 *sqq.*: improvements in bank at, 148: finance at, 146 *sqq.*: address from British inhabitants to Wellesley, 164.
CANNING, Rt. Hon. George, Wellesley's sympathy with, 170: makes Wellesley Foreign Secretary, 172: 176, 182.
CASTLEREAGH, Viscount, on treaty of Bassein, 87 *sqq.*: criticism on Wellesley's policy, 100: on private trade, 154: letters to Wellesley, 142, 155: Wellesley's letters to, 109, 147: suicide, 182.
CEYLON, its union with Bombay suggested, 113: its government and defence, 132–133, 135: Mr. North, Governor of, 133.
CLIVE, second Lord, Governor of Madras, Wellesley writes to him, 28, 60: cordial relations with Wellesley, 29: with Mr. Webbe, 156: Wellesley's instructions to him, 134: retirement, 159.
CLOSE, Colonel, 48, 59, 85.
COLLEGE at Fort William, 119 *sqq.*
COLLINS, Colonel, 93.
CORNWALLIS, Marquess, his ac-

quaintance with Wellesley, 17: his acceptance of the Governor-Generalship a second time, but continuance in Ireland, 18: reversal of Wellesley's policy, 108: returns as Governor-General, 108, 164.
CRAIG, Sir James, commands in Oudh, 64: his opinion of Nawáb's troops, 65: on defence of N. W., 136: letter of, 137.

DE BOIGNE, General, 96-97.
DEOGÁON, treaty of, 96.
DHUNDIA WÁGH, 45.
DÍG, 107.
DUNDAS, Rt. Hon. H., Viscount Melville, influence over Wellesley, 20, 22: letters to Wellesley, 27, 64, 66, 139: instructions to Wellesley, 33, 59: Wellesley's letters to, 63, 117, 133, 134, 138: comments on Wellesley's suggestions, 115: on monopoly, 151, 154: letter from, 149.

EDMONSTONE, Neil, 59.

FOX, Rt. Hon. C. J., 79.
FRAZER, General, 103.

GÁEKWÁR, the, 86, 136.
GARRICK, David, his compliment to Wellesley, 14: Wellesley compared to, 19.
GEORGE, Prince of Wales, 169, 174, 175.
GOODALL, Dr., his opinion of Wellesley's scholarship, 13.
GORE, Hon. Charles, 184, 186 note.
GRANT, Mr., on private trade, 152.
GRATTAN, Wellesley's admiration for, 15 and note.
GRENVILLE, William, Lord, at school with Wellesley, 14: Chief Secretary for Ireland, 14: Wellesley's letters to him, 14, 15: consulted by Pitt, 165; grief at Pitt's death, 168: his protest with Wellesley, 177.
GREVILLE MEMOIRS, 186-187.

HAIDAR ALÍ, 24, 32, 58.
HARCOURT, Colonel, 3.
HARRIS, General, afterwards Lord, at Madras, 36: his correspondence with Wellesley, 36 sqq.: takes command of the army, 43: begins siege of Seringapatam, 44: sends gift to Wellesley, 53.
HASTINGS, first Marquess of, 106.
HASTINGS, Warren, his approval of Wellesley's educational scheme, 122-124: referred to, 11, 20.
HOBART, Lord, 18, 21, 28, 58 note, 133.
HOLKAR, Jeswant Ráo, 84, 85, 86, 87, 90, 93: war with, 99 sqq.: his cruelty, 100: his successful strategy, 101-102: his power crushed, 108.
HOLKAR, Túkají Ráo, 33, 84-85.

IMTIAZ UL DAULAH, 34.

JONES, Sir William, 121.

KARNÁTIK, Wellesley's policy towards, 56-61.
KIRKPATRICK, James Achilles, 22, 23, 24.
KIRKPATRICK, William, 69, 156.

LASWÁRI, battle of, 97.
LUCKNOW, 67, 75, 169.
LUMSDEN, Mr., 66.

MADRAS, Arthur Wellesley goes out to, 17: Mornington appointed Governor, 18: Lord Macartney ex-Governor of, 21: fear of Tipú at, 24: the Government and Council of, 27-29: the timid officials at, 36: congratulations from, 51: proposals concerning, 113 sqq.: finance at, 146.
MALARTIE, Governor of Mauritius, his proclamation, 35-36.
MALCOLM, Sir John, assistant at Haidarábád, 25: Arthur Wel-

lesley's letters to, 91 : sent to Persia, 129.
MAURITIUS, the Tipú's negotiations with, 35 : expedition against planned, 130-131 : French fleet sails to, 134.
MAXWELL, Lieutenant, 95.
MILL, James, *History of British India*, criticism on Wellesley, 39-40 : argues on behalf of Muhammad Alí, 59 : criticises Wellesley's policy with regard to the Nawábs, 61 : on treaty of Bassein, 88-89 : praises Wellesley's sagacity, 155.
MONSON, Colonel Hon. William, his force, 101 : his disaster, 102-104 : its causes and results, 104-106, 108, 163.
MUHAMMAD ALÍ, Nawáb of the Karnátik, 58 *sqq*.
MUHAMMAD AMIR KHÁN, Memoirs, 101.
MURRAY, Colonel, 101, 102 : takes Indore, 106.
MYSORE, conquest of, 43-45 : settlement of, 45-49 : its prosperity, 50-51 : Northern frontier in British hands, 27 : power of, 33.
MYSORE, Hindú Rájás of, 41, 47, 48, 49, 50.

NÁNA FARNAVIS, 43, 83 : his policy and death, 84.
NEWPORT, Sir John, 14.
NIZÁM, the, Wellesley's policy towards, 22-27.

OMDAL UL OMRAH, 58, 60.
OUDH, 33, 40, 49, 64 *sqq*., 136, 157.
OUSELEY, Sir Gore, 129.
OWEN, Mr. Sidney, 56 *note*, 86, 92 *note*, 146 *note*.

PALMER, Colonel, British Resident at Poona, 42, 84, 85.
PARR, Dr. Samuel, 13.
PAULL, Mr., attacks Wellesley, 168-169.
PEEL, Sir Robert, 186, 188.
PERCEVAL, Rt. Hon. S., 176.

PERRON, General, at Haidarábád, 26 : in Hindustán, 89 and *note*, 96, 134 : his defeat, retirement, and character, 97, 128.
PESHWÁ, Bájí Rao, 83, 85 *sqq.*, 93.
PITT, William, Wellesley's support of and intimacy with, 15-16 : correspondence with Wellesley, 55 : attitude towards proprietors, 79 : his friendship for, 165-166 : his last letter to Wellesley, 167 : his last interview and death, 168.
PITT, William, Earl of Chatham, 203.
POORNEAH, influence in Mysore, 50.

RAINIER, Admiral, 131 *sqq*.
RAYMOND, General, 22, 23, 26, 34.
ROBERTS, Colonel, 26.

SAÁDAT ALÍ, Nawáb Wázir of Oudh, 68 *et seqq*.
SARAGOSSA, maid of, 171 *note*.
SARBOJÍ, Rájá of Tanjore, 62.
SÁTÁRA, Rájá of, 92.
SCHWARZ, Danish missionary, 62.
SCOTT, Colonel, Resident at Lucknow, 69, 73, 74, 75.
SEVILLE, Wellesley at, 171.
SHÁH 'ALÁM, the Mughal Emperor, 89 *note*, 94, 97, 98, 127, 128.
SHORE, Sir John, Lord Teignmouth, 18, 20, 28, 66, 68.
SINDHIA, Daulat Ráo, youth, 33 : threatened by rebellion, 83 : in Marátha war, 85 *sqq*. : views of treaty of Bassein, 92, 93 : defeated at Delhi and Laswári, 97 : signs treaty, 98 : his troops desert Monson, 104 : throws off English alliance, 106.
SINDHIA MAHADÁJÍ, his power, 33, 83 : his army, 96.
SPAIN, Wellesley in, 170-172.
STEPHEN, Sir James Fitzjames, 21.
STEVENSON, Colonel, 94.
STEWART, General, 43 : on Indian defence, 134 *sqq*. : power delegated to, 158.

STRACHEY, Sir John, 21.
SURAT, settlement of, 63, 64.
SURJÍ ARJANGÁON treaty, 98.

TANJORE, settlement of, 62-63, 64, 73.
TIPÚ SULTÁN, danger from him, 24: his barbarity, 31: at the peace of Mangalore, 32: associated with Zemán Sháh, 34: his position in 1798, 34-35: sends envoys to Mauritius, 35: attack on him directed, 37: his letters, 38 *sqq.*: the war against him, 42 *sqq.*: Mill's defence of him, 39-40: his death, 44 and *note*: his children, 44-45: his jewels, 53: relations with Nawáb, 58-60.
TUCKER, H. St. George, 145: receives control of finance, 147: his plan for Bank of Calcutta, 148: his Memoirs, ib. *note*.

UDNY, Mr., on private trade, 152.
UMJID UL DAULAH, 34.

VALENTIA, Lord, his travels in India, 31 *note*.

WARNAK RÁO, Peshwá, 85.
WEBBE, Josiah, memorandum on Mysore, 36: examines letters of Nizám, 59: his removal, 156.
WELLESLEY, Arthur, Duke of Wellington, birth, 13: at Eton, 14: goes out to India, 17: his letters, 18: his opinion of the Bombay administration, 30: head of Commission to treat with subjects of Tipú, 41: defeats Dhundia Wágh, 45: on Commission in Mysore, 48: his opinion of the settlement, 50-51: memorandum on state of India quoted, 57, 58, 80, 145: on Karnátik, 57, 58: on Oudh settlement, 80: answer to Castlereagh, 89: on the subsidiary treaties, 91, 92: political agent at Poona, 93: war in the Deccan, 94: victory at Assaye, 94-95: storms Gáwilgarh, 96: signs treaty of Deogáon, 96: begins war with Holkar, 101: judgement on Monson's defeat, 102, 104, 105: on Lake, 107: on Indian defence, 134, 141: on Indian affairs, 145-146: on monopoly, 150: delegation of power to Generals Wellesley and Stewart submitted to counsel's opinion, 159: receives Order of the Bath, 163: letter from Stowe, 165: advice on attack on his brother, 166: created Viscount Wellington, 172: retreat to Portugal, 172: victory in Spain, 177: made a Marquess, 177: breach with his brother, 184: reconciliation with, 190.
WELLESLEY, Rev. Henry, son of the Marquess, 167.
WELLESLEY, Henry, Lord Cowley, 13, 20, 25: on Commission in Mysore, 48: in Oudh, 75, 157, 158: his success, 75-76: his removal, 78-79: subsequent career, 79: appointed ambassador to Spain, 172.
WELLESLEY, first Marchioness of, 166-167, 187: second Marchioness of, 187.
WELLESLEY, Richard, son of the Marquess, 167, 172.
WELLESLEY, Richard Colley, Earl of Mornington and Marquess Wellesley, birth, 13: at Harrow, 13: at Eton, 13: his school friends, 14: at Oxford, 14: succeeds his father, 14: in the Irish House of Lords, 14, 15: in English House of Commons, 15: his political views, 16-17: his interest in India, 17-18: appointed Governor-General and made a peer of Great Britain, 18: his embarkation, 19: his freedom from personal interest, 20: at the Cape of Good Hope, 21: letters on the Nizám, 22-23: his policy to-

wards Nizám, 24-27 : relations with Madras Governor and Council, 28-29 : with Bombay, 29 : sketches the position in Mysore, 34-35 : determines on war, 36 : preliminaries, 37-39 : charges against him, 39-40 : letter to General Harris, 41-42 : settlement of Mysore, 45-48 : his great success, 48-49 : congratulations and gifts, 51-54 : made Captain-General, 54 : Marquess of Wellesley, 55 : letter to the Nawáb, settlement of the Karnátik, 60 : of Tanjore, 62-63 : of Surat, 63 : of Oudh, 64-81 : appointment of his brother Henry criticized, 79, 80 : charges against, 77-78 : his estimate on the Marátha problem, 82-83 : the treaty of Bassein, 85 : his objects in Marátha war, 93 : his reply to congratulations on the success of the war, 99 : negotiations with Holkar, 100-101 : letters from Lake, 102-103 : his generosity to Monson, 105 : Monson's defeat the final blow to his position, 106 : justification of his territorial acquisitions, 108-110 : his minute on the government, 111-113 : a MS. paper of his, 113-115 : his ideal of Indian government, 116-117 : his opinion of the Company's civil servants, 117-119 : 'Notes on foundation of College,' 119-121 : its foundation, 122 : his religious policy, 124-127 : his defensive policy, 127 : relations with the Mughal Emperor, 128 : with Persia, 129 : Red Sea Expedition, 130 : plans defeated by Rainier, 131 : letter to him, 131-132 : his views on Ceylon, 132-133 : his bold action with regard to French possessions, Goa and Serampur, 134 : demand for increase of troops, 138 : disgust at the Directors' blindness, 141 : increase of troops, 142 : his financial policy, 144-148 : on private trade, 148-154 : a disciple of Adam Smith, 150 : use of patronage, 154-156 : charges against him, 157-159 : resignation, 159 : consents to remain, 160 : letter from, 160 *sqq.*: letter to Castlereagh on the Court of Directors, 163 : Cornwallis appointed his successor, 163 : returns to England, 164 : disappointments in domestic life, 166, 167 : letter from Pitt, 167-168 : grief at Pitt's death, 168 : attack on Wellesley, 169 : return to public life, he turns to foreign affairs, 169-170 : sympathy with Canning, 170 : political views, 170 : Ambassador-Extraordinary to Spain, 170 : reception in Seville, 171 : his difficulties, 171 : appointed Foreign Secretary and receives Order of Garter, 172 : his speech on the Spanish war, 172-173 : political zeal and views, 174 *sqq.* : gives up the seals, 175 : in Ireland as Lord Lieutenant, 179-183 : character of his rule, 183 : resignation and breach with Wellington, 184 *sqq.*: made Lord Steward of the Household, 186 : Lord Lieutenant of Ireland again, 186 : Lord Chamberlain, 186 : retirement, 186 : last years, 187-190 : publication of his Indian despatches, 189 : acts of atonement by Directors, 189 : reconciliation with his brother, 190 : death, 190 : personal appearance of, 193 : portraits of, 193 *sqq.*: ill-health, 195-196 : conversational powers, 196 : literary taste, 188, 196-198 : personal character, 198 *sqq.*

WELLESLEY, William, Earl of Maryborough and of Mornington, 12, 165.

WESLEY, Anne, Countess of Mornington, 12, 13.
WESLEY, Charles, declined to be adopted by Garret Wesley, 12.
WESLEY, Garret, 12.
WESLEY, Garret, first Earl of Mornington, 12.
WESLEY, Richard Colley, Baron Mornington, 12.
WESTMORELAND, Lord, 200.
WILBERFORCE, Wellesley in agreement with him on the slave trade, 16: his diary mentions Wellesley, 17: his opinion of Wellesley's character, 205.

ZALÍM SINGH, 103.
ZEMÁN SHÁH, fear of invasion from, 33, 65: associated with Tipú, 34, 65: the Doáb regarded as a protection against Zemán Sháh, 67: Persian treaty arranged as protection against, 129.

THE END.

RULERS OF INDIA:

THE CLARENDON PRESS SERIES OF INDIAN HISTORICAL RETROSPECTS.

Edited by SIR W. W. HUNTER, K.C.S.I., M.A., LL.D.

The following 26 volumes have been published:—

I. *A BRIEF HISTORY OF THE INDIAN PEOPLES*, by SIR WILLIAM WILSON HUNTER, K.C.S.I. Twenty-second Edition; 84th thousand. Price 3s. 6d.

II. *AKBAR: and the Rise of the Mughal Empire*, by COLONEL MALLESON, C.S.I., Author of *A History of the Indian Mutiny; The History of Afghanistan.* Fifth thousand. 2s. 6d.

III. *ALBUQUERQUE: and the Early Portuguese Settlements in India*, by H. MORSE STEPHENS, Esq., M.A., Balliol College, Lecturer on Indian History at Cambridge, Author of *The French Revolution; The Story of Portugal, &c.* 2s. 6d.

IV. *AURANGZÍB: and the Decay of the Mughal Empire*, by STANLEY LANE POOLE, Esq., B.A., Author of *The Coins of the Mughal Emperors; The Life of Stratford Canning; Catalogue of Indian Coins in the British Museum, &c.* 2s. 6d.

V. *MADHAVA RAO SINDHIA: and the Hindú Reconquest of India*, by H. G. KEENE, Esq., M.A., C.I.E., Author of *The Moghul Empire, &c.* 2s. 6d.

VI. *LORD CLIVE: and the Establishment of the English in India*, by COLONEL MALLESON, C.S.I. 2s. 6d.

VII. *DUPLEIX: and the Struggle for India by the European Nations*, by COLONEL MALLESON, C.S.I., Author of *The History of the French in India, &c.* Fourth thousand. 2s. 6d.

VIII. *WARREN HASTINGS: and the Founding of the British Administration*, by CAPTAIN L. J. TROTTER, Author of *India under Victoria, &c.* Fifth thousand. 2s. 6d.

IX. *THE MARQUESS CORNWALLIS: and the Consolidation of British Rule*, by W. S. SETON-KARR, Esq., sometime Foreign Secretary to the Government of India, Author of *Selections from the Calcutta Gazettes*, 3 vols. (1784-1805). Third thousand. 2s. 6d.

X. *HAIDAR ALÍ AND TIPÚ SULTÁN: and the Struggle with the Muhammadan Powers of the South*, by LEWIN BENTHAM BOWRING, Esq., C.S.I., sometime Private Secretary to the Viceroy (Lord Canning) and Chief Commissioner of Mysore, Author of *Eastern Experiences.* 2s. 6d.

XI. *THE MARQUESS WELLESLEY: and the Development of the Company into the Supreme Power in India*, by the Rev. W. H. HUTTON, M.A., Fellow and Tutor of St. John's College, Oxford. 2s. 6d.

XII. *THE MARQUESS OF HASTINGS: and the Final Overthrow of the Maráthá Power*, by MAJOR ROSS OF BLADENSBURG, C.B., Coldstream Guards; F.R.G.S. 2s. 6d.

RULERS OF INDIA SERIES (*continued*).

XIII. *MOUNTSTUART ELPHINSTONE: and the Making of South-Western India*, by J. S. COTTON, Esq., M.A., formerly Fellow of Queen's College, Oxford, Author of *The Decennial Statement of the Moral and Material Progress and Condition of India*, presented to Parliament (1885), &c. 2s. 6d.

XIV. *SIR THOMAS MUNRO: and the British Settlement of the Madras Presidency*, by JOHN BRADSHAW, Esq., M.A., LL.D., Inspector of Schools, Madras. 2s. 6d.

XV. *EARL AMHERST: and the British Advance eastwards to Burma*, chiefly from unpublished papers of the Amherst family, by Mrs. ANNE THACKERAY RITCHIE, Author of *Old Kensington, &c.*, and RICHARDSON EVANS, Esq. 2s. 6d.

XVI. *LORD WILLIAM BENTINCK: and the Company as a Governing and Non-trading Power*, by DEMETRIUS BOULGER, Esq., Author of *England and Russia in Central Asia; The History of China, &c.* 2s. 6d.

XVII. *EARL OF AUCKLAND: and the First Afghan War*, by CAPTN. L. J. TROTTER, Author of *India under Victoria*. 2s. 6d.

XVIII. *VISCOUNT HARDINGE: and the Advance of the British Dominions into the Punjab*, by his Son and Private Secretary, the Right Hon. VISCOUNT HARDINGE. Third thousand. 2s. 6d.

XIX. *RANJIT SINGH: and the Sikh Barrier between our Growing Empire and Central Asia*, by SIR LEPEL GRIFFIN, K.C.S.I., Author of *The Punjab Chiefs, &c.* Third thousand. 2s. 6d.

XX. *JOHN RUSSELL COLVIN: the last Lieutenant-Governor of the North-Western Provinces under the Company*, by his son, SIR AUCKLAND COLVIN, K.C.S.I., late Lieutenant-Governor of the North-Western Provinces. 2s. 6d.

XXI. *THE MARQUESS OF DALHOUSIE: and the Final Development of the Company's Rule*, by SIR WILLIAM WILSON HUNTER, K.C.S.I., M.A. Seventh thousand. 2s. 6d.

XXII. *CLYDE AND STRATHNAIRN: and the Suppression of the Great Revolt*, by MAJOR-GENERAL SIR OWEN TUDOR BURNE, K.C.S.I., sometime Military Secretary to the Commander-in-Chief in India. Fourth thousand. 2s. 6d.

XXIII. *EARL CANNING: and the Transfer of India from the Company to the Crown*, by SIR HENRY S. CUNNINGHAM, K.C.I.E., M.A., Author of *British India and its Rulers, &c.* Third thousand. 2s. 6d.

XXIV. *LORD LAWRENCE: and the Reconstruction of India under the Crown*, by SIR CHARLES UMPHERSTON AITCHISON, K.C.S.I., LL.D., formerly Foreign Secretary to the Government of India, and Lieutenant-Governor of the Punjab. Fourth thousand. 2s. 6d.

XXV. *THE EARL OF MAYO: and the Consolidation of the Queen's Rule in India*, by SIR WILLIAM WILSON HUNTER, K.C.S.I., M.A., LL.D. Third thousand. 2s. 6d.

SUPPLEMENTARY VOLUME.

XXVI. *JAMES THOMASON: and the British Settlement of North-Western India*, by SIR RICHARD TEMPLE, Bart., M.P., formerly Lieutenant-Governor of Bengal, and Governor of Bombay. Price 3s. 6d.

The Clarendon Press History of India, 3s. 6d.

A BRIEF HISTORY OF THE INDIAN PEOPLES.

STANDARD EDITION (TWENTY-SECOND), REVISED TO 1895.
EIGHTY-FOURTH THOUSAND.

This Edition incorporates the suggestions received by the author from Directors of Public Instruction and other educational authorities in India; its statistics are brought down to the Census of 1891; and its narrative to 1892. The work has received the emphatic approval of the organ of the English School Boards, and has been translated into five languages. It is largely employed for educational purposes in Europe and America and as a text-book prescribed by the University of Calcutta for its Entrance Examination from 1886 to 1891.

'"A Brief History of the Indian Peoples," by W. W. Hunter, presents a sort of bird's-eye view both of India and of its people from the earliest dawn of historical records. . . . A work of authority and of original value.'—*The Daily News* (London).

' Dr. Hunter may be said to have presented a compact epitome of the results of his researches into the early history of India; a subject upon which his knowledge is at once exceptionally wide and exceedingly thorough.'—*The Scotsman.*

' Within the compass of some 250 pages we know of no history of the people of India so concise, so interesting, and so useful for educational purposes as this.'—*The School Board Chronicle* (London).

' For its size and subject there is not a better written or more trustworthy history in existence.'—*The Journal of Education.*

' So thoroughly revised as to entitle it to separate notice.'—*The Times.*

' Dr. Hunter's history, if brief, is comprehensive. It is a storehouse of facts marshalled in a masterly style; and presented, as history should be, without the slightest suspicion of prejudice or suggestion of partisanship. Dr. Hunter observes a style of severe simplicity, which is the secret of an impressive presentation of details.'—*The Daily Review* (Edinburgh).

' By far the best manual of Indian History that has hitherto been published, and quite equal to any of the Historical Series for Schools edited by Dr. Freeman. We trust that it will soon be read in all the schools in this Presidency.'—*The Times of India.*

Extract from a criticism by Edward Giles, Esq., Inspector of Schools, Northern Division, Bombay Presidency:—' What we require is a book which shall be accurate as to facts, but not overloaded with them; written in a style which shall interest, attract, and guide uncultivated readers; and short, because it must be sold at a reasonable price. These conditions have never, in my opinion, been realized previous to the introduction of this book.'

' The publication of the Hon. W. W. Hunter's "School History of India" is an event in literary history.'—*Reis & Rayyet* (Calcutta).

' He has succeeded in writing a history of India, not only in such a way that it will be read, but also in a way which we hope will lead young Englishmen and young natives of India to think more kindly of each other. The Calcutta University has done wisely in prescribing this brief history as a text-book for the Entrance Examination.'—*The Hindoo Patriot* (Calcutta).

Opinions of the Press
ON
SIR WILLIAM HUNTER'S 'DALHOUSIE.'

'An interesting and exceedingly readable volume..... Sir William Hunter has produced a valuable work about an important epoch in English history in India, and he has given us a pleasing insight into the character of a remarkable Englishman. The "Rulers of India" series, which he has initiated, thus makes a successful beginning in his hands with one who ranks among the greatest of the great names which will be associated with the subject.'—*The Times.*

'To no one is the credit for the improved condition of public intelligence [regarding India] more due than to Sir William Hunter. From the beginning of his career as an Indian Civilian he has devoted a rare literary faculty to the task of enlightening his countrymen on the subject of England's greatest dependency. ... By inspiring a small army of fellow-labourers with his own spirit, by inducing them to conform to his own method, and shaping a huge agglomeration of facts into a lucid and intelligible system, Sir W. Hunter has brought India and its innumerable interests within the pale of achievable knowledge, and has given definite shape to the truths which its history establishes and the problems which it suggests.... Such contributions to literature are apt to be taken as a matter of course, because their highest merit is to conceal the labour, and skill, and knowledge involved in their production; but they raise the whole level of public intelligence, and generate an atmosphere in which the baleful influences of folly, ignorance, prejudice, and presumption dwindle and disappear.'—*Saturday Review.*

'Admirably calculated to impart in a concise and agreeable form a clear general outline of the history of our great Indian Empire.'—*Economist.*

'A skilful and most attractive picture.... The author has made good use of public and private documents, and has enjoyed the privilege of being aided by the deceased statesman's family. His little work is, consequently, a valuable contribution to modern history.'—*Academy.*

'The book should command a wide circle of readers, not only for its author's sake and that of its subject, but partly at least on account of the very attractive way in which it has been published at the moderate price of half-a-crown. But it is, of course, by its intrinsic merits alone that a work of this nature should be judged. And those merits are everywhere conspicuous.... A writer whose thorough mastery of all Indian subjects has been acquired by years of practical experience and patient research.'—*The Athenæum.*

'Never have we been so much impressed by the great literary abilities of Sir William Hunter as we have been by the perusal of "The Marquess of Dalhousie."... The knowledge displayed by the writer of the motives of Lord Dalhousie's action, of the inner working of his mind, is so complete, that Lord Dalhousie himself, were he living, could not state them more clearly.... Sir William Hunter's style is so clear, his language so vivid, and yet so simple, conveying the impressions he wishes so perspicuously that they cannot but be understood, that the work must have a place in every library, in every home, we might say indeed every cottage.'—*Evening News.*

'Sir William Hunter has written an admirable little volume on "The Marquess of Dalhousie" for his series of the "Rulers of India." It can be read at a sitting, yet its references—expressed or implied—suggest the study and observation of half a life-time.'—*The Daily News.*

Opinions of the Press
ON
SIR WILLIAM HUNTER'S 'LORD MAYO.'

'Sir William W. Hunter has contributed a brief but admirable biography of the Earl of Mayo to the series entitled "Rulers of India," edited by himself (Oxford, at the Clarendon Press).'—*The Times.*

'In telling this story in the monograph before us, Sir William Hunter has combined his well-known literary skill with an earnest sympathy and fulness of knowledge which are worthy of all commendation. . . . The world is indebted to the author for a fit and attractive record of what was eminently a noble life.'—*The Academy.*

'The sketch of The Man is full of interest, drawn as it is with complete sympathy, understanding, and appreciation. But more valuable is the account of his administration. No one can show so well and clearly as Sir William Hunter does what the policy of Lord Mayo contributed to the making of the Indian Empire of to-day.'—*The Scotsman.*

'Sir William Hunter has given us a monograph in which there is a happy combination of the essay and the biography. We are presented with the main features of Lord Mayo's administration unencumbered with tedious details which would interest none but the most official of Anglo-Indians; while in the biography the man is brought before us, not analytically, but in a life-like portrait.'—*Vanity Fair.*

'The story of his life Sir W. W. Hunter tells in well-chosen language —clear, succinct, and manly. Sir W. W. Hunter is in sympathy with his subject, and does full justice to Mayo's strong, genuine nature. Without exaggeration and in a direct, unaffected style, as befits his theme, he brings the man and his work vividly before us.'—*The Glasgow Herald.*

'All the knowledge acquired by personal association, familiarity with administrative details of the Indian Government, and a strong grasp of the vast problems to be dealt with, is utilised in this presentation of Lord Mayo's personality and career. Sir W. Hunter, however, never overloads his pages, and the outlines of the sketch are clear and firm.' —*The Manchester Express.*

'This is another of the "Rulers of India" series, and it will be hard to beat. . . . Sir William Hunter's perception and expression are here at their very best.'—*The Pall Mall Gazette.*

'The latest addition to the "Rulers of India" series yields to none of its predecessors in attractiveness, vigour, and artistic portraiture. . . . The final chapter must either be copied verbally and literally—which the space at our disposal will not permit—or be left to the sorrowful perusal of the reader. The man is not to be envied who can read it with dry eyes.'—*Allen's Indian Mail.*

'The little volume which has just been brought out is a study of Lord Mayo's career by one who knew all about it and was in full sympathy with it. . . . Some of these chapters are full of spirit and fire. The closing passages, the picture of the Viceroy's assassination, cannot fail to make any reader hold his breath. We know what is going to happen, but we are thrilled as if we did not know it, and were still held in suspense. The event itself was so terribly tragic that any ordinary description might seem feeble and laggard. But in this volume we are made to feel as we must have felt if we had been on the spot and seen the murderer "fastened like a tiger" on the back of the Viceroy.'—*Daily News*, Leading Article.

Opinions of the Press

ON

MR. W. S. SETON-KARR'S 'CORNWALLIS.'

'This new volume of the "Rulers of India" series keeps up to the high standard set by the author of "The Marquess of Dalhousie." For dealing with the salient passages in Lord Cornwallis's Indian career no one could have been better qualified than the whilom foreign secretary to Lord Lawrence.'—*The Athenæum*.

'We hope that the volumes on the "Rulers of India" which are being published by the Clarendon Press are carefully read by a large section of the public. There is a dense wall of ignorance still standing between the average Englishman and the greatest dependency of the Crown; although we can scarcely hope to see it broken down altogether, some of these admirable biographies cannot fail to lower it a little. . . . Mr. Seton-Karr has succeeded in the task, and he has not only presented a large mass of information, but he has brought it together in an attractive form. . . . We strongly recommend the book to all who wish to enlarge the area of their knowledge with reference to India.'—*New York Herald*.

'We have already expressed our sense of the value and timeliness of the series of Indian historical retrospects now issuing, under the editorship of Sir W. W. Hunter, from the Clarendon Press. It is somewhat less than fair to say of Mr. Seton-Karr's monograph upon Cornwallis that it reaches the high standard of literary workmanship which that series has maintained.'—*The Literary World*.

MRS. THACKERAY RITCHIE'S AND MR. RICHARDSON EVANS'

'LORD AMHERST.'

'The story of the Burmese War, its causes and its issues, is re-told with excellent clearness and directness.'—*Saturday Review*.

'Perhaps the brightest volume in the valuable series to which it belongs. . . . The chapter on "The English in India in Lord Amherst's Governor-Generalship" should be studied by those who wish to understand how the country was governed in 1824.'—*Quarterly Review*.

'There are some charming pictures of social life, and the whole book is good reading, and is a record of patience, skill and daring. The public should read it, that it may be chary of destroying what has been so toilsomely and bravely acquired.'—*National Observer*.

'The book will be ranked among the best in the series, both on account of the literary skill shown in its composition and by reason of the exceptional interest of the material to which the authors have had access.'—*St. James's Gazette*.

Opinions of the Press
ON
MR. S. LANE-POOLE'S 'AURANGZÍB.'

'There is no period in Eastern history so full of sensation as the reign of Aurangzíb. ... Mr. Lane-Poole tells this story admirably; indeed, it were difficult to imagine it better told.'—*National Observer.*

'Mr. Lane-Poole writes learnedly, lucidly, and vigorously. ... He draws an extremely vivid picture of Aurangzíb, his strange ascetic character, his intrepid courage, his remorseless overthrow of his kinsmen, his brilliant court, and his disastrous policy; and he describes the gradual decline of the Mogul power from Akbar to Aurangzíb with genuine historical insight.'—*Times.*

'A well-knit and capable sketch of one of the most remarkable, perhaps the most interesting, of the Mogul Emperors.'—*Saturday Review.*

'As a study of the man himself, Mr. Lane-Poole's work is marked by a vigour and originality of thought which give it a very exceptional value among works on the subject.'—*Glasgow Herald.*

'The most popular and most picturesque account that has yet appeared ... a picture of much clearness and force.'—*Globe.*

'A notable sketch, at once scholarly and interesting.'—*English Mail.*

'No one is better qualified than Mr. Stanley Lane-Poole to take up the history and to depict the character of the last of the great Mogul monarchs. ... Aurangzíb's career is ever a fascinating study.'—*Home News.*

'The author gives a description of the famous city of Sháh Jahán, its palaces, and the ceremonies and pageants of which they were the scene. ... Mr. Lane-Poole's well-written monograph presents all the most distinctive features of Aurangzíb's character and career.'—*Morning Post.*

MAJOR ROSS OF BLADENSBURG'S 'MARQUESS OF HASTINGS.'

'Major Ross of Bladensburg treats his subject skilfully and attractively, and his biography of Lord Hastings worthily sustains the high reputation of the Series in which it appears.'—*The Times.*

'This monograph is entitled to rank with the best of the Series, the compiler having dealt capably and even brilliantly with his materials.'—*English Mail.*

'Instinct with interest.'—*Glasgow Evening News.*

'As readable as it is instructive.'—*Globe.*

'A truly admirable monograph.'—*Glasgow Herald.*

'Major Ross has done his work admirably, and bids fair to be one of the best writers the Army of our day has given to the country. ... A most acceptable and entrancing little volume.'—*Daily Chronicle.*

'It is a volume that merits the highest praise. Major Ross of Bladensburg has represented Lord Hastings and his work in India in the right light, faithfully described the country as it was, and in a masterly manner makes one realize how important was the period covered by this volume.'—*Manchester Courier.*

'This excellent monograph ought not to be overlooked by any one who would fully learn the history of British rule in India.'—*Manchester Examiner.*

Opinions of the Press

ON

COLONEL MALLESON'S 'DUPLEIX.'

'In the character of Dupleix there was the element of greatness that contact with India seems to have generated in so many European minds, French as well as English, and a broad capacity for government, which, if suffered to have full play, might have ended in giving the whole of Southern India to France. Even as it was, Colonel Malleson shows how narrowly the prize slipped from French grasp. In 1783 the Treaty of Versailles arrived just in time to save the British power from extinction.'—*Times.*

'One of the best of Sir W. Hunter's interesting and valuable series. Colonel Malleson writes out of the fulness of familiarity, moving with ease over a field which he had long ago surveyed in every nook and corner. To do a small book as well as this on Dupleix has been done, will be recognised by competent judges as no small achievement. When one considers the bulk of the material out of which the little volume has been distilled, one can still better appreciate the labour and dexterity involved in the performance.'—*Academy.*

'A most compact and effective history of the French in India in a little handbook of 180 pages.'—*Nonconformist.*

'Well arranged, lucid and eminently readable, an excellent addition to a most useful series.'—*Record.*

COLONEL MALLESON'S 'AKBAR.'

'Colonel Malleson's interesting monograph on Akbar in the "Rulers of India" (Clarendon Press) should more than satisfy the general reader. Colonel Malleson traces the origin and foundation of the Mughal Empire; and, as an introduction to the history of Muhammadan India, the book leaves nothing to be desired.'—*St. James's Gazette.*

'This volume will, no doubt, be welcomed, even by experts in Indian history, in the light of a new, clear, and terse rendering of an old, but not worn-out theme. It is a worthy and valuable addition to Sir W. Hunter's promising series.'—*Athenæum.*

'Colonel Malleson has broken ground new to the general reader. The story of Akbar is briefly but clearly told, with an account of what he was and what he did, and how he found and how he left India. . . . The native chronicles of the reign are many, and from them it is still possible, as Colonel Malleson has shown, to construct a living portrait of this great and mighty potentate.'—*Scots Observer.*

'The brilliant historian of the Indian Mutiny has been assigned in this volume of the series an important epoch and a strong personality for critical study, and he has admirably fulfilled his task. . . . Alike in dress and style, this volume is a fit companion for its predecessor.'—*Manchester Guardian.*

Opinions of the Press
ON
CAPTAIN TROTTER'S 'WARREN HASTINGS.'

'The publication, recently noticed in this place, of the "Letters, Despatches, and other State Papers preserved in the Foreign Department of the Government of India, 1772–1785," has thrown entirely new light from the most authentic sources on the whole history of Warren Hastings and his government of India. Captain L. J. Trotter's WARREN HASTINGS is accordingly neither inopportune nor devoid of an adequate *raison d'être*. Captain Trotter is well known as a competent and attractive writer on Indian history, and this is not the first time that Warren Hastings has supplied him with a theme.'—*The Times*.

'He has put his best work into this memoir.... His work is of distinct literary merit, and is worthy of a theme than which British history presents none nobler. It is a distinct gain to the British race to be enabled, as it now may, to count the great Governor-General among those heroes for whom it need not blush.'—*Scotsman*.

'Captain Trotter has done his work well, and his volume deserves to stand with that on Dalhousie by Sir William Hunter. Higher praise it would be hard to give it.'—*New York Herald*.

'Captain Trotter has done full justice to the fascinating story of the splendid achievements of a great Englishman.'—*Manchester Guardian*.

'A brief but admirable biography of the first Governor-General of India.'—*Newcastle Chronicle*.

'A book which all must peruse who desire to be "up to date" on the subject.'—*The Globe*.

MR. KEENE'S 'MADHAVA RAO SINDHIA.'

'Mr. Keene has the enormous advantage, not enjoyed by every producer of a book, of knowing intimately the topic he has taken up. He has compressed into these 203 pages an immense amount of information, drawn from the best sources, and presented with much neatness and effect.'—*The Globe*.

'Mr. Keene tells the story with knowledge and impartiality, and also with sufficient graphic power to make it thoroughly readable. The recognition of Sindhia in the "Rulers" series is just and graceful, and it cannot fail to give satisfaction to the educated classes of our Indian fellow-subjects.'—*North British Daily Mail*.

'The volume bears incontestable proofs of the expenditure of considerable research by the author, and sustains the reputation he had already acquired by his "Sketch of the History of Hindustan."'—*Freeman's Journal*.

'Among the eighteen rulers of India included in the scheme of Sir William Hunter only five are natives of India, and of these the great Madhoji Sindhia is, with the exception of Akbar, the most illustrious. Mr. H. G. Keene, a well-known and skilful writer on Indian questions, is fortunate in his subject, for the career of the greatest bearer of the historic name of Sindhia covered the exciting period from the capture of Delhi, the Imperial capital, by the Persian Nadir Shah, to the occupation of the same city by Lord Lake. ... Mr. Keene gives a lucid description of his subsequent policy, especially towards the English when he was brought face to face with Warren Hastings.'—*The Daily Graphic*.

Opinions of the Press

ON

MAJOR-GENERAL SIR OWEN BURNE'S 'CLYDE AND STRATHNAIRN.'

'In "Clyde and Strathnairn," a contribution to Sir William Hunter's excellent "Rulers of India" series (Oxford, at the Clarendon Press), Sir Owen Burne gives a lucid sketch of the military history of the Indian Mutiny and its suppression by the two great soldiers who give their names to his book. The space is limited for so large a theme, but Sir Owen Burne skilfully adjusts his treatment to his limits, and rarely violates the conditions of proportion imposed upon him.' ... 'Sir Owen Burne does not confine himself exclusively to the military narrative. He gives a brief sketch of the rise and progress of the Mutiny, and devotes a chapter to the Reconstruction which followed its suppression.' ... '— well written, well proportioned, and eminently worthy of the series to which it belongs.'—*The Times.*

'Sir Owen Burne who, by association, experience, and relations with one of these generals, is well qualified for the task, writes with knowledge, perspicuity, and fairness.'—*Saturday Review.*

'As a brief record of a momentous epoch in India this little book is a remarkable piece of clear, concise, and interesting writing.'—*The Colonies and India.*

'Sir Owen Burne has written this book carefully, brightly, and with excellent judgement, and we in India cannot read such a book without feeling that he has powerfully aided the accomplished editor of the series in a truly patriotic enterprise.'—*Bombay Gazette.*

'The volume on "Clyde and Strathnairn" has just appeared, and proves to be a really valuable addition to the series. Considering its size and the extent of ground it covers it is one of the best books about the Indian Mutiny of which we know.'—*Englishman.*

'Sir Owen Burne, who has written the latest volume for Sir William Hunter's "Rulers of India" series, is better qualified than any living person to narrate, from a military standpoint, the story of the suppression of the Indian Mutiny.'—*Daily Telegraph.*

'Sir Owen Burne's book on "Clyde and Strathnairn" is worthy to rank with the best in the admirable series to which it belongs.'—*Manchester Examiner.*

'The book is admirably written; and there is probably no better sketch, equally brief, of the stirring events with which it deals.'—*Scotsman.*

'Sir Owen Burne, from the part he played in the Indian Mutiny, and from his long connexion with the Government of India, and from the fact that he was military secretary of Lord Strathnairn both in India and in Ireland, is well qualified for the task which he has undertaken.'—*The Athenæum.*

Opinions of the Press

ON

VISCOUNT HARDINGE'S 'LORD HARDINGE.'

'An exception to the rule that biographies ought not to be entrusted to near relatives. Lord Hardinge, a scholar and an artist, has given us an accurate record of his father's long and distinguished services. There is no filial exaggeration. The author has dealt with some controversial matters with skill, and has managed to combine truth with tact and regard for the feelings of others.'—*The Saturday Review.*

'This interesting life reveals the first Lord Hardinge as a brave, just, able man, the very soul of honour, admired and trusted equally by friends and political opponents. The biographer ... has produced a most engaging volume, which is enriched by many private and official documents that have not before seen the light.'—*The Anti-Jacobin.*

'Lord Hardinge has accomplished a grateful, no doubt, but, from the abundance of material and delicacy of certain matters, a very difficult task in a workmanlike manner, marked by restraint and lucidity.'—*The Pall Mall Gazette.*

'His son and biographer has done his work with a true appreciation of proportion, and has added substantially to our knowledge of the Sutlej Campaign.'—*Vanity Fair.*

'The present Lord Hardinge is in some respects exceptionally well qualified to tell the tale of the eventful four years of his father's Governor-Generalship.'—*The Times.*

'It contains a full account of everything of importance in Lord Hardinge's military and political career; it is arranged ... so as to bring into special prominence his government of India; and it gives a lifelike and striking picture of the man.'—*Academy.*

'The style is clear, the treatment dispassionate, and the total result a manual which does credit to the interesting series in which it figures.'—*The Globe.*

'The concise and vivid account which the son has given of his father's career will interest many readers.'—*The Morning Post.*

'Eminently readable for everybody. The history is given succinctly, and the unpublished letters quoted are of real value.'—*The Colonies and India.*

'Compiled from public documents, family papers, and letters, this brief biography gives the reader a clear idea of what Hardinge was, both as a soldier and as an administrator.'—*The Manchester Examiner.*

'An admirable sketch.'—*The New York Herald.*

'The Memoir is well and concisely written, and is accompanied by an excellent likeness after the portrait by Sir Francis Grant.'—*The Queen.*

Opinions of the Press
ON
SIR HENRY CUNNINGHAM'S 'EARL CANNING.'

'Sir Henry Cunningham's rare literary skill and his knowledge of Indian life and affairs are not now displayed for the first time, and he has enjoyed exceptional advantages in dealing with his present subject. Lord Granville, Canning's contemporary at school and colleague in public life and one of his oldest friends, furnished his biographer with notes of his recollections of the early life of his friend. Sir Henry Cunningham has also been allowed access to the Diary of Canning's private secretary, to the Journal of his military secretary, and to an interesting correspondence between the Governor-General and his great lieutenant, Lord Lawrence.'—*The Times.*

'Sir H. S. Cunningham has succeeded in writing the history of a critical period in so fair and dispassionate a manner as to make it almost a matter of astonishment that the motives which he has so clearly grasped should ever have been misinterpreted, and the results which he indicates so grossly misjudged. Nor is the excellence of his work less conspicuous from the literary than from the political and historical point of view.'—*Glasgow Herald.*

'Sir H. S. Cunningham has treated his subject adequately. In vivid language he paints his word-pictures, and with calm judicial analysis he also proves himself an able critic of the actualities, causes, and results of the outbreak, also a temperate, just appreciator of the character and policy of Earl Canning.'—*The Court Journal.*

REV. W. H. HUTTON'S 'MARQUESS WELLESLEY.'

'Mr. Hutton has brought to his task an open mind, a trained historical judgement, and a diligent study of a great body of original material. Hence he is enabled to present a true, authentic, and original portrait of one of the greatest of Anglo-Indian statesmen, doing full justice to his military policy and achievements, and also to his statesmanlike efforts for the organization and consolidation of that Empire which he did so much to sustain.'—*Times.*

'To the admirable candour and discrimination which characterize Mr. Hutton's monograph as an historical study must be added the literary qualities which distinguish it and make it one of the most readable volumes of the series. The style is vigorous and picturesque, and the arrangement of details artistic in its just regard for proportion and perspective. In short, there is no point of view from which the work deserves anything but praise.'—*Glasgow Herald.*

'The Rev. W. H. Hutton has done his work well, and achieves with force and lucidity the task he sets himself: to show how, under Wellesley, the Indian company developed and ultimately became the supreme power in India. To our thinking his estimate of this great statesman is most just.'—*Black and White.*

'Mr. Hutton has told the story of Lord Wellesley's life in an admirable manner, and has provided a most readable book.'—*Manchester Examiner.*

'Mr. Hutton's range of information is wide, his division of subjects appropriate, and his diction scholarly and precise.'—*Saturday Review.*

Opinions of the Press

ON

SIR LEPEL GRIFFIN'S 'RANJIT SINGH.'

'We can thoroughly praise Sir Lepel Griffin's work as an accurate and appreciative account of the beginnings and growth of the Sikh religion and of the temporal power founded upon it by a strong and remorseless chieftain.'—*The Times.*

'Sir Lepel Griffin treats his topic with thorough mastery, and his account of the famous Mahárájá and his times is, consequently, one of the most valuable as well as interesting volumes of the series of which it forms a part.'—*The Globe.*

'From first to last it is a model of what such a work should be, and a classic.'—*The St. Stephen's Review.*

'The monograph could not have been entrusted to more capable hands than those of Sir Lepel Griffin, who spent his official life in the Punjaub.'—*The Scotsman.*

'At once the shortest and best history of the rise and fall of the Sikh monarchy.'—*The North British Daily Mail.*

'Not only a biography of the Napoleon of the East, but a luminous picture of his country; the chapter on Sikh Theocracy being a notable example of compact thought.'—*The Liverpool Mercury.*

MR. DEMETRIUS BOULGER'S 'LORD WILLIAM BENTINCK.'

'The "Rulers of India" series has received a valuable addition in the biography of the late Lord William Bentinck. The subject of this interesting memoir was a soldier as well as a statesman. He was mainly instrumental in bringing about the adoption of the overland route and in convincing the people of India that a main factor in English policy was a disinterested desire for their welfare. Lord William's despatches and minutes, several of which are textually reproduced in Mr. Boulger's praiseworthy little book, display considerable literary skill and are one and all State papers of signal worth.'—*Daily Telegraph.*

'Mr. Boulger is no novice in dealing with Oriental history and Oriental affairs, and in the career of Lord William Bentinck he has found a theme very much to his taste, which he treats with adequate knowledge and literary skill.'—*The Times.*

'Mr. Boulger writes clearly and well, and his volume finds an accepted place in the very useful and informing series which Sir William Wilson Hunter is editing so ably.'—*Independent.*

Opinions of the Press

ON

MR. J. S. COTTON'S 'MOUNTSTUART ELPHINSTONE.'

'Sir William Hunter, the editor of the series to which this book belongs, was happily inspired when he entrusted the Life of Elphinstone, one of the most scholarly of Indian rulers, to Mr. Cotton, who, himself a scholar of merit and repute, is brought by the nature of his daily avocations into close and constant relations with scholars. ... We live in an age in which none but specialists can afford to give more time to the memoirs of even the most distinguished Anglo-Indians than will be occupied by reading Mr. Cotton's two hundred pages. He has performed his task with great skill and good sense. This is just the kind of Life of himself which the wise, kindly, high-souled man, who is the subject of it, would read with pleasure in the Elysian Fields.'—Sir M. E. Grant Duff, in *The Academy*.

'To so inspiring a theme few writers are better qualified to do ample justice than the author of "The Decennial Statement of the Moral and Material Progress and Condition of India." Sir T. Colebrooke's larger biography of Elphinstone appeals mainly to Indian specialists, but Mr. Cotton's slighter sketch is admirably adapted to satisfy the growing demand for a knowledge of Indian history and of the personalities of Anglo-Indian statesmen which Sir William Hunter has done so much to create.'—*The Times*.

DR. BRADSHAW'S 'SIR THOMAS MUNRO.'

'A most valuable, compact and interesting memoir for those looking forward to or engaged in the work of Indian administration.'—*Scotsman*.

'It is a careful and sympathetic survey of a life which should always serve as an example to the Indian soldier and civilian.'—*Yorkshire Post*.

'A true and vivid record of Munro's life-work in almost autobiographical form.'—*Glasgow Herald*.

'Of the work before us we have nothing but praise. The story of Munro's career in India is in itself of exceptional interest and importance.'—*Freeman's Journal*.

'The work could not have been better done; it is a monument of painstaking care, exhaustive research, and nice discrimination.'—*People*.

'This excellent and spirited little monograph catches the salient points of Munro's career, and supplies some most valuable quotations from his writings and papers.'—*Manchester Guardian*.

'It would be impossible to imagine a more attractive and at the same time instructive book about India.'—*Liverpool Courier*.

'It is one of the best volumes of this excellent series.'—*Imperial and Asiatic Quarterly Review*.

'The book throughout is arranged in an admirably clear manner and there is evident on every page a desire for truth, and nothing but the truth.'—*Commerce*.

'A clear and scholarly piece of work.'—*Indian Journal of Education*.

Opinions of the Press

ON

MR. MORSE STEPHENS' 'ALBUQUERQUE.'

'Mr. Stephens' able and instructive monograph ... We may commend Mr. Morse Stephens' volume, both as an adequate summary of an important period in the history of the relations between Asia and Europe, and as a suggestive treatment of the problem of why Portugal failed and England succeeded in founding an Indian Empire.'—*The Times.*

'Mr. H. Morse Stephens has made a very readable book out of the foundation of the Portuguese power in India. According to the practice of the series to which it belongs it is called a life of Affonso de Albuquerque, but the Governor is only the central and most important figure in a brief history of the Portuguese in the East down to the time when the Dutch and English intruded on their preserves ... A pleasantly-written and trustworthy book on an interesting man and time.' —*The Saturday Review.*

'Mr. Morse Stephens' *Albuquerque* is a solid piece of work, well put together, and full of interest.'—*The Athenæum.*

'Mr. Morse Stephens' studies in Indian and Portuguese history have thoroughly well qualified him for approaching the subject ... He has presented the facts of Albuquerque's career, and sketched the events marking the rule of his predecessor Almeida, and of his immediate successors in the Governorship and Viceroyalty of India in a compact, lucid, and deeply interesting form.'—*The Scotsman.*

SIR CHARLES AITCHISON'S 'LORD LAWRENCE.'

'No man knows the policy, principles, and character of John Lawrence better than Sir Charles Aitchison. The salient features and vital principles of his work as a ruler, first in the Punjab, and afterwards as Viceroy, are set forth with remarkable clearness.'— *Scotsman.*

'A most admirable sketch of the great work done by Sir John Lawrence, who not only ruled India, but saved it.'—*Manchester Examiner.*

'Sir Charles Aitchison's narrative is uniformly marked by directness, order, clearness, and grasp; it throws additional light into certain nooks of Indian affairs; and it leaves upon the mind a very vivid and complete impression of Lord Lawrence's vigorous, resourceful, discerning, and valiant personality.'—*Newcastle Daily Chronicle.*

'Sir Charles knows the Punjab thoroughly, and has made this little book all the more interesting by his account of the Punjab under John Lawrence and his subordinates.'—*Yorkshire Post.*

Opinions of the Press

ON

LEWIN BENTHAM BOWRING'S 'HAIDAR ALÍ AND TIPÚ SULTÁN.'

'Mr. Bowring's portraits are just, and his narrative of the continuous military operations of the period full and accurate.'—*Times.*

'The story has been often written, but never better or more concisely than here, where the father and son are depicted vividly and truthfully "in their habit as they lived." There is not a volume of the whole series which is better done than this, or one which shows greater insight.'—*Daily Chronicle.*

'Mr. Bowring has been well chosen to write this memorable history, because he has had the best means of collecting it, having himself formerly been Chief Commissioner of Mysore. The account of the Mysore war is well done, and Mr. Bowring draws a stirring picture of our determined adversary.'—*Army and Navy Gazette.*

'An excellent example of compression and precision. Many volumes might be written about the long war in Mysore, and we cannot but admire the skill with which Mr. Bowring has condensed the history of the struggle. His book is as terse and concise as a book can be.'—*North British Daily Mail.*

'Mr. Bowring's book is one of the freshest and best of a series most valuable to all interested in the concerns of the British Empire in the East.'—*English Mail.*

'The story of the final capture of Seringapatam is told with skill and graphic power by Mr. Bowring, who throughout the whole work shows himself a most accurate and interesting historian.'—*Perthshire Advertiser.*

COLONEL MALLESON'S 'LORD CLIVE.'

'This book gives a spirited and accurate sketch of a very extraordinary personality.'—*Speaker.*

'Colonel Malleson writes a most interesting account of Clive's great work in India—so interesting that, having begun to read it, one is unwilling to lay it aside until the last page has been reached. The character of Clive as a leader of men, and especially as a cool, intrepid, and resourceful general, is ably described; and at the same time the author never fails to indicate the far-reaching political schemes which inspired the valour of Clive and laid the foundation of our Indian Empire.'—*North British Daily Mail.*

'This monograph is admirably written by one thoroughly acquainted and in love with his subject.'—*Glasgow Herald.*

'No one is better suited than Colonel Malleson to write on Clive, and he has performed his task with distinct success. The whole narrative is, like everything Colonel Malleson writes, clear and full of vigour.'—*Yorkshire Post.*

'Colonel Malleson is reliable and fair, and the especial merit of his book is that it always presents a clear view of the whole of the vast theatre in which Clive gradually produces such an extraordinary change of scene.'—*Newcastle Daily Chronicle.*

Opinions of the Press

ON

CAPT. TROTTER'S 'EARL OF AUCKLAND.'

'A vivid account of the causes, conduct, and consequences of "the costly, fruitless, and unrighteous" Afghan War of 1838.'—*St. James's Gazette.*

'To write such a monograph was a thankless task, but it has been accomplished with entire success by Captain L. J. Trotter. He has dealt calmly and clearly with Lord Auckland's policy, domestic and military, with its financial results, and with the general tendency of Lord Auckland's rule.'—*Yorkshire Post.*

'To this distressing story (of the First Afghan War) Captain Trotter devotes the major portion of his pages. He tells it well and forcibly; but is drawn, perhaps unavoidably, into the discussion of many topics of controversy which, to some readers, may seem to be hardly as yet finally decided. . . . It is only fair to add that two chapters are devoted to "Lord Auckland's Domestic Policy," and to his relations with "The Native States of India." '—*The Times.*

'Captain Trotter's *Earl of Auckland* is a most interesting book, and its excellence as a condensed, yet luminous, history of the first Afghan War deserves warm recognition.'—*Scotsman.*

'It points a moral which our Indian Rulers cannot afford to forget so long as they still have Russia and Afghanistan to count with.'—*Glasgow Herald.*

Supplementary Volume: price 3s. 6d.

'JAMES THOMASON,' BY SIR RICHARD TEMPLE.

'Sir R. Temple's book possesses a high value as a dutiful and interesting memorial of a man of lofty ideals, whose exploits were none the less memorable because achieved exclusively in the field of peaceful administration.'—*Times.*

'It is the peculiar distinction of this work that it interests a reader less in the official than in the man himself.'—*Scotsman.*

'This is a most interesting book: to those who know India, and knew the man, it is of unparalleled interest, but no one who has the Imperial instinct which has taught the English to rule subject races "for their own welfare" can fail to be struck by the simple greatness of this character.'—*Pall Mall Gazette.*

'Mr. Thomason was a great Indian statesman. He systematized the revenue system of the North-West Provinces, and improved every branch of the administration. He was remarkable, like many great Indians, for the earnestness of his religious faith, and Sir Richard Temple brings this out in an admirable manner.'—*British Weekly.*

'The book is "a portrait drawn by the hand of affection," of one whose life was "a pattern of how a Christian man ought to live." Special prominence is given to the religious aspects of Mr. Thomason's character, and the result is a very readable biographical sketch.'—*Christian.*

Opinions of the Press

ON

SIR AUCKLAND COLVIN'S 'JOHN RUSSELL COLVIN.'

'The concluding volume of Sir William Hunter's admirable "Rulers of India" series is devoted to a biography of John Russell Colvin. Mr. Colvin, as private secretary to Lord Auckland, the Governor-General during the first Afghan War, and as Lieutenant-Governor of the North-West Provinces during the Mutiny, bore a prominent part in the government of British India at two great crises of its history. His biographer is his son, Sir Auckland Colvin, who does full justice to his father's career and defends him stoutly against certain allegations which have passed into history.... It is a valuable and effective contribution to an admirable series. In style and treatment of its subject it is well worthy of its companions.'—*Times.*

'Sir Auckland Colvin has been able to throw new light on many of the acts of Lord Auckland's administration, and on the state of affairs at Agra on the outbreak of the Mutiny.... This memoir will serve to recall the splendid work which Colvin really performed in India, and to exhibit him as a thoroughly honourable man and conscientious ruler.'—*Daily Telegraph.*

'This book gives an impressive account of Colvin's public services, his wide grasp of native affairs, and the clean-cut policy which marked his tenure of power.'—*Leeds Mercury.*

'The story of John Colvin's career indicates the lines on which the true history of the first Afghan War and of the Indian Mutiny should be written.... Not only has the author been enabled to make use of new and valuable material, but he has also constructed therefrom new and noteworthy explanations of the position of affairs at two turning-points in Indian history.'—*Academy.*

'High as is the standard of excellence attained by the volumes of this series, Sir Auckland Colvin's earnest work has reached the high-water mark.'—*Army and Navy Gazette.*

'Sir Auckland Colvin has done his part with great tact and skill. As an example of the clear-sighted way in which he treats the various Indian problems we may cite what he says on the education of the natives—a question always of great moment to the subject of this biography.'—*Manchester Guardian.*

'Sir Auckland Colvin gives us an admirable study of his subject, both as a man of affairs and as a student in private life. In doing this, his picturesque theme allows him, without outstepping the biographical limits assigned, to present graphic pictures of old Calcutta and Indian life in general.'—*Manchester Courier.*

'This little volume contains pictures of India, past and present, which it would be hard to match for artistic touch and fine feeling. We wish there were more of the same kind to follow.'—*St. James's Gazette.*

'The monograph is a valuable addition to a series of which we have more than once pointed out the utility and the excellence.'—*Glasgow Herald.*